Faithfully Prescribed

Copyright © 2017 by **Alan Fūss**

All rights reserved. This book or any portion thereof may not be reproduced or used in any manner whatsoever without the express written permission of the publisher except for the use of brief quotations in a book review.

Printed in the United States of America

First Printing, 2017

ISBN 978-0692796047

Table of Contents

Forewords	5
Preface: The macron and Ross Hunter	7
Dedication	9
Introduction	10
How I Got Here	15
"Alan, you should be a minister"	17
How did this occur? Was this God's plan, or simply mine?	22
The gift of inspiration	27
Unusual occurrences	31
Near misses (x6)	46
Inspired by a movie	53
My secret mentor	56
Getting excited about a trip	57
Belief and Prayer	61
Bold proclamation!	63
The purpose of worshipping God	64
Judeo-Christianity	65
The case for church	69
In (spiritual) fact(s), I have faith!	71
Crumbs from the table	75
A faith of convenience?	76
Promotion by demotion	77
Predestination vs. free will, and the Elect	80
Things of this world	83
Things best left to God	85
Why do we do good works?	89
"Enough, already!!!"	91
The Holy Trinity	96
A few words about Satan	103
My thoughts on the Lord's Prayer	104
My prayers	108
Looking for a sign?	120

Science and Related Topics	121
The value of science	123
Creation and evolution	125
Physics of faith (and a little chemistry and math)	134
Time	138
Public Life	141
Government and politics	143
Render unto Caesar	155
Living Our Faith	163
Ancient wisdom	165
There's power in them thar words!	168
Could I be part of the problem?	171
Reflections on spigotology	177
Proud of our faith?	181
Long-term investing	183
Limited by our success	185
Living one's faith as a medical professional	187
How to live	194
The Prescription	202
Afterwords	205
Toward a full disclosure	207
Whom would I like to meet?	212
What's next?	216
Some good words	216

Forewords

Preface: The macron and Ross Hunter

You may have noticed the line over the letter u in my name. This line is called a macron. In case you are wondering, I had no idea that the line to which I am referring is called a macron until I did a little research. I am using a macron over the u in my last name to indicate that we are still using the German pronunciation of Fuss (the u is pronounced like oo in goose or moose). We haven't adopted the English pronunciation.

The connection to Ross Hunter takes a little longer to explain. When I was in high school, my trigonometry teacher told me about seeing Ross Hunter, a movie producer, the previous night on The Tonight Show. She told me about Johnny Carson asking Ross Hunter what his name was before it was changed to Ross Hunter. It was Martin Terry Fuss. My teacher asked me if I was related to him. I told her that I had no idea. This was in the days before the internet, so my ability to learn more about Ross Hunter was very limited.

About twenty to twenty-five years later, a nurse in the ER told me that she had recently seen a movie in which one of the characters was Dr. Fuss. At first, I thought that she was kidding me. She was serious, however. She told me the name of the movie. It was Magnificent Obsession. I watched the listings in the paper to see when this movie would be on TV again. Finally, I found that it would be on one of the classic movie channels. I watched it. Indeed, there was a Dr. Fuss in the movie; I think that his full name was Dr. Albert Fuss. He was a Swiss neurologist who was consulted by one of the main characters. Just before the viewers were introduced to Dr. Fuss, they were shown his name at the entry to his office; his last name was spelled the same as mine and the pronunciation was the same. What I found to be equally intriguing was the name of the producer, listed in the credits. The producer was Ross Hunter.

I found that our library had the book version of Magnificent Obsession. I quickly paged through it, but could find no mention of Dr. Fuss. In the book, the doctor had a different last name. I immediately concluded that Ross Hunter (Martin Terry Fuss) was trying to use his movie to make moviegoers aware of the preferred pronunciation of Fuss.

Dedication

I dedicate this book to you, my readers, in the hope that you will benefit from reading what I have written. I also dedicate these pages to my wife, sons, daughters-in-law, and grandchildren. And, just as I did in the version that I wrote for my family, I am dedicating this to You, God. Your position at the end of the list is meant to serve as a reminder of my frequent failures to keep You as Number One.

Introduction

From the Fall of 2015 through the Spring of 2016, I wrote a book for my family. The title was *Stories of Family and Faith*. My initial inspiration for writing came from recalling a series of three unusual events that I experienced over a period lasting approximately twenty years beginning in the early 1990s and ending on April 29, 2011. After I had begun to write for my family, I experienced two additional unusual events that served as further inspiration to continue this project.

For me, these events have been faith strengthening; my hope is that they can and will do the same for you. Without these unusual events, I am quite certain that I wouldn't have done this writing, or anything resembling it. I consider these events not only my inspiration to write, but also my credentials to write, however unearned those credentials may be.

Two reasons guided my decision to write the family stories for my family. First, I felt that they would help "explain" me; I had this vague sense that I needed to be "explained." The second reason was that for a long time, I have wished that I knew more about my ancestors, especially what they were like and what they thought about. I felt that if I desired this type of information for myself, I should be providing it for my descendants.

Writing the family stories helped me finish a journey of self-enlightenment. A couple of months before starting to write, I began to realize that I had actually been on this journey for much of my life. It turned out that the only one who actually needed to have me "explained" was me! The essence of my self-enlightenment is that after retirement, I came to understand that I have probably had slight depression most of my life, and that my brother had suffered mild to moderate depression – and sometimes far worse – for most of his life.

During my career in medicine, I had felt at times that I was experiencing work related burnout, and didn't give any real thought to possible depression. Now, after looking back closely at my childhood, I realize that our parents' bad marriage was the source of the depression my brother and I shared. Although we were always treated well by our parents, throughout our childhood, adolescence, and teenage years we witnessed them fighting frequently. It was depressing, to say the least. But despite their frequent fights, both of our parents were wonderful people, and there are countless people who would be envious of our childhood. We both loved our parents, and we wouldn't have traded them for any other. Here is my first bit of advice – my first prescription – to you, the reader: if you and your spouse must argue in front of your children, be sure to do so in a constructive, civil and even mildly spirited manner, but whatever you do, please don't fight with your spouse in a way that frightens or depresses your children!

So why this book, and why now?

Traditionally, the spiritual leader of the family has been the husband and father. This tradition seems to be deteriorating in modern times, and I confess that I fell short in this area. I usually tried to set a good example by attempting to "live my faith," but my examples weren't always good. I think that wives and mothers make equally good spiritual leaders; often they are much better. My mother was certainly the spiritual leader of our home when I was growing up. Sometimes I thought that she was too much of a spiritual leader, but I no longer think that way…

My initial objective was simply to record the stories of the unusual events I mention above, but as I began writing, it quickly turned into something bigger and deeper. It became a way for me to create a record of my faith and beliefs, and about my perceptions of God. It also became a way to help me provide some of the spiritual leadership for my family that I should have provided years earlier.

It quickly became clear that my ultimate goal in writing about my faith is, to borrow one of my pastor's favorite expressions, "to increase the population of Heaven!" I want to see all of you there!

While writing for my family, I began to realize that never before in my life had I experienced anywhere near as much joy, inspiration, and peace from something "work related." When I completed the writing, I actually had mixed feelings. On the one hand, I was happy to be done, but on the other, I was somewhat saddened that the feelings of joy, inspiration, and peace had decreased.

The closer I got to completing my faith stories, as I like to call them, the more I felt that my writing might be worth sharing with a much larger audience beyond my family. After I completed the book for my family, I felt as though I were in limbo about the decision of whether to publish the faith stories. Would my writing be acceptable enough to God?

All I could do was pray about the decision. "Dear Lord, please help me with this decision. Please give me some sort of more definite input about whether to publish." Then, within a couple of days, I most definitely noticed an absolutely awful feeling of dissatisfaction when I was in the mindset of not publishing; it was moderate depression and a complete lack of peace. This feeling was worse than anything I had experienced during my medical career. I knew that I had to get away from this feeling! When I began to think more positively about publishing, the joy and peace returned, and there was no feeling of depression. That was enough of a sign for me! It was at that point that I decided to go ahead with the publishing project.

By now, you might be wondering whether I am some kind of religious nut. If this is what you're thinking, then you are absolutely right! I think that I always have been "some kind of religious nut", but until recently I never felt comfortable writing about it or talking about it. I think that God should be the Number One Priority in our lives, and that our faith should be the most important thing in our minds. Our faith has profound implications, not only for our life on earth, but also for our eternal life!

Although it may not seem that way to some, at least initially, I think that my faith and beliefs are consistent with what God (the Holy Trinity) teaches us in the Bible. Most of what I write about my faith and beliefs has probably been addressed before. St. Augustine, for example, wrote extensively on time and eternity centuries ago. But some of what I write is surely new. I am writing from the perspective of an ordinary Christian, rather from that of a theologian pretender. Of course, theologians would immediately be aware that I am not a theologian, and they should be aware that I am not pretending to be one, either.

For years, I have prayed for a simple but strong faith, but in March 2016, I began praying for a simple, strong, and childlike faith. I started doing this when it became clear to me that one shouldn't need the knowledge of a theologian to adequately understand our faith and beliefs. I base this thought on the words of Jesus in Matthew 18:3, "Verily I say unto you, Except ye be converted and become like little children, ye shall not enter the kingdom of Heaven."·

· Throughout this book, I use the King James Version (KJV) of the Bible for the simple reason that I have always been fond of the language and style in that version. Readers should feel free to use any translation of the Bible that they feel brings them closest to the Word of God.

In keeping with a simple, strong, and childlike faith, I think that we need to focus our faith energy on learning and understanding the necessary, core beliefs of Christianity, and incorporating those beliefs into our heart, mind, and soul. As we do that, we need to intertwine the childlike qualities of love and trust amongst the other components of our faith. Then, we need to focus on preserving our faith, including the elements of love and trust. We should spend some time and effort learning and understanding other very interesting, but less important, parts of our faith; these can help reinforce our core beliefs. "The Prescription" appearing later in this book will list the necessary actions and core beliefs of our faith. If you believe nothing else that I write, at least believe this part!

What I have written in this book is an accurate representation of my faith and beliefs. As I learn more from the Bible, I may change my mind about certain things that I have written, but I don't expect that there will be much change. For ten to fifteen years, at least, I have periodically prayed: "Dear Lord, If my current faith isn't the true faith, please inspire me with the true faith." The basics of my faith and beliefs haven't changed, but in the past ten to fifteen years I have been blessed by a much greater awareness that our God (the Holy Trinity) is a very loving God.

At various stages of this project, including well before I ever started writing, I have occasionally thought about what God might think of me. I suspect that one thing He thought was, "What will it take to get Alan to talk about His faith?......An act of God???"

Of course, I absolutely believe that God always knew this and that He might have been urging me all along, through the Holy Spirit, in the same way a parent urges a two-year-old to talk: "Alan, use your words!!! Use your words!!!"

Well, here are my words!

How I Got Here

"Alan, you should be a minister"

From the time I was in the fourth or fifth grade until eighth or ninth grade, my mom would frequently tell me, "Alan, you should be a minister." She also urged my brother, Marvin, to do the same, but I remember her saying it more to me. I would always answer something like, "No, I don't think so," or, "No, I don't want to." I always assumed that she was saying this just because of her faith zeal. But now I often wonder, "Did mom see something in me that I didn't recognize, or didn't allow myself to recognize?"

We frequently listened to various radio ministries – at home, in the car or in our pickup truck. Mom was always the one who would tune the radio to the right station for these programs. And she always seemed to know exactly when they'd be on. She was particularly fond of three programs. One was Billy Graham's radio ministry, "The Hour of Decision." Another was the radio ministry of the Lutheran Church, Missouri Synod called "The Lutheran Hour." The third was "The World Tomorrow" (see "Enough, already" for my recollections of this program).

I was always so impressed with the ministers who preached on these programs. Billy Graham was so eloquent with his rich tenor voice and North Carolina accent. In those days, I didn't know that his accent was connected with North Carolina; I just thought that he sounded pretty cool. And his message was very inspiring!

The minister of The Lutheran Hour was the Reverend Doctor Oswald Hoffmann. Just his name and title by themselves were awe inspiring. And his voice was so commanding! His voice was deeper than Billy Graham's. And he didn't sound as passionate as Billy Graham, but he didn't need to! His delivery was calm, quietly inspiring, but also commanding and confident. In his case, too much passion would have been overdoing it, it would have been wasted effort! He was so self-assured and authoritative that I would often think, "This must be like listening to Martin Luther, himself!" Recently, I changed the previous thought to "mostly Martin Luther, blended with a little of General Patton." And the powerful organ music before and after his message, namely, "A Mighty Fortress Is Our God," reinforced his message and added to my sense of awe.

I suspect that mom noted how quiet and attentive I was when these men were speaking. But had I been asked what my thoughts were, I would have never knowingly betrayed my awe of them. Recently, I realized that one of my former coworkers, a nurse, may have answered why mom repeatedly suggested that I become a minister. He told me that I have an expressive face. I knew that I didn't have a poker face, but I told him that I didn't think that my face was all that expressive. He then replied something like, "Dr. Fuss, I don't think I have ever known anyone else with such an expressive face!" Maybe my thoughts had to come out in some manner, and when I didn't allow them to come out as spoken words, they forced their way out as facial expressions. So now I think that because of my face, mom could sense my awe of these ministers.

I think that part of my awe of these men came from my sense that I would never be that eloquent and commanding myself. Sometimes I would have brief fantasies about being such a speaker, but they never lasted very long. While reading a passage in Exodus last year, I found that the thoughts of Moses echoed how I felt then and still feel about speaking. In Exodus 4:10, in the early stages of God calling him to lead His people from Egypt, we find Moses' reply, "O my Lord, I am not eloquent, neither heretofore, nor since thou hast spoken unto Thy servant: but I am slow of speech, and of a slow tongue." I might not be quite as bad as Moses describes himself, but I have always felt at least something similar when it comes to speaking. I do not enjoy public speaking and have generally done what I can to avoid it!

Not only was I in awe of the radio ministers, I was comfortable in the church. I especially liked the large sanctuaries with stained glass. I liked the organ music and the service itself. But I would never have admitted this to anyone until I was far into adulthood.

A little more than fifteen years after I last heard anything from my mom about becoming a minister, I experienced the first of four interesting events that kept this memory alive. During our years in Fremont, on one of my visits to the ER to see a patient, a nurse told me an interesting story. She told me of an adult patient who had been in the ER the night before, intoxicated. When he was asked who HIS doctor was, he replied, "Father Fuss." With further questioning it was determined that I was the doctor for his child. The story made me laugh. But I would occasionally wonder why he had answered in this manner. I would wonder if he thought, consciously or subconsciously, that I acted like a priest.

Years later, I received an advertisement from a car dealership in the mail. The advertisement was unusual in one regard; it had been addressed to Rev. Alan Fuss. Probably a simple mistake.

A few years ago, I was visiting an injured relative in the hospital. Our fathers were first cousins. We hadn't seen each other since childhood, and while we really didn't know each other, we knew about each other. Something in our conversation led him to say, "I thought you were a minister."

The last reminder occurred in late September 2014 during a residency reunion in San Francisco. The main purpose of the reunion was to honor the wishes of J, who was dying of cancer. J finished his medical residency training a year ahead of me. Seeing him again, and seeing how he was facing death in such a dignified and gracious manner was inspirational to me. But the reason that I include this story now is my conversation with H, another friend who was in J's group. H is Jewish, and while we were speaking I told him that I had discovered that I might have some Jewish roots. He then said something interesting, something along the lines of, "I can imagine you descending from a long line of rabbis."

Occasionally, I would think of these little stories with amusement. Probably all were meaningless. But, in the past several months, especially considering my current subject matter, I started thinking, "Hmmmm?....Did God, in a humorous manner, keep the embers glowing a little? Hmmmm?

Direct Call

I have a fond childhood memory of returning home from a movie I had seen with my entire family. Maybe what makes me remember this so well was that my parents were laughing together at one of the lines of the movie, for they rarely shared any laughter just between themselves. I'm fairly sure that the movie was *Spencer's Mountain*. The line was part of a conversation between two characters who were discussing a new minister who had recently come to serve in their church. The line that made my parents laugh, which I didn't fully understand at that time, went something like "Is he ordained, or did he get his call direct?"

I would occasionally think of that line in the years since then, and I frequently think about it now. And I especially think this way now in regard to my writing, "I'm certainly not ordained; instead, my call was direct." Despite my call being spread out over many years, I still think of it as direct. And what did my call consist of? I think that it consisted of my mother's repeated advice that I should become a minister, the feelings that I would get with news of Middle Eastern conflicts (see "Enough, already!"), the occasional references to me being like a minister or a rabbi, and, especially, the experiences I write about in 'Unusual occurrences', culminating in the 3 AM Awakening. I was already well into this project when I had the 3 AM Awakening, but for a few weeks prior to that experience, I had relaxed in my efforts (due to travel, family visits, and being sick). I now think of the 3 AM Awakening in three ways. First, I think that God was telling me something like the following: "OK, you've had your rest, and you've recovered. Now it's time to get back to work!" Second, I believe it validated my efforts to that point; it made me feel that I am on the right track. Finally, it energized my call; it converted its wattage from that of a nightlight to that of a searchlight!

How did this occur? Was this God's plan, or simply mine?

I started thinking about this a little once when I had the 3 AM awakening that I have told you about. And I started thinking about it a lot more in late March and early April 2016 when I was aware that my inspiration level and work-related joy were increasing.

Regardless of whose plan it was (God's or mine), God has always known that I would be writing this, just as He has always known that you would be reading this. This thought, plus the fact that He gave me several unusual experiences that confirmed His existence to me, experiences that He knew I would ultimately be writing about, make me feel comfortable in saying that God is okay with what I am writing. In fact, I have the feeling that it was His plan all along!

Why would God want me to write this book, considering that some parts are probably controversial, especially my thoughts on humans evolving before the creation of Adam and Eve? I think that it is precisely because of this and other possibly controversial parts that He inspired me to write! For three reasons, I believe that He wanted someone, through writing, to reconcile science, including evolution, and faith. One reason is the widespread understanding of, and appreciation for, science, including evolution, that people now have. The second is the widespread perception of conflict between our faith and science, especially evolutionary science. And the third reason is that this perception of conflict between faith and science is likely preventing a number of people from fully embracing their faith in God, or entirely preventing them from being able to receive a spark of faith at all. He has always known that there would be a need to reconcile science and faith. For this particular task, He needed someone with a good knowledge and appreciation of science and also a strong faith (there were other requirements for other parts of the book; I will address all of the requirements for this book, as I see them, below). And I feel that His judgment and plan required me to do this writing, and to do it now.

Regardless of whose plan it was, writing this book came with the following requirements:

I needed to develop a comfort, and even a love, for deep thought and reflection that wouldn't require interruption from the "real world" around me. During my adolescence and teenage years, my shyness, low self-esteem, social unease, and even my hearing loss probably all helped me to become very comfortable with spending long periods of time in thought, without interruption. And a mildly depressed mind might have an advantage regarding deep thought; with our slower processing, those of us with mildly depressed minds aren't as apt to dismiss ideas too quickly.

I needed to learn about people. This was a long process, because, due to my circumstances growing up, I was socially naïve and socially awkward when I left my parents' home. Meeting my wife was the start of this process. She has always had much more people wisdom than I have had, but I'm getting closer to her level. And there is not a better career in which to learn about people than the medical profession. And within the medical profession, I doubt if there is a better place in which to learn about people than a pediatric emergency department.

I needed to learn about one person in particular – myself! This would help me uncover the slight depression that I have likely always had and that needed to be at least partially overcome for me to get on with this project fully.

In early retirement, after my post-retirement euphoria wore off, and before this project started, I had the feeling that something wasn't quite right, which led to the feeling that I should start looking at my past in depth, especially my childhood. This was occurring while I started making plans to record the stories of my unusual events, at least for my family. As the idea to write a small book, based mainly on these stories, took shape, it struck me that it should include family stories. But why? Mainly because I felt the need to explain myself, to show where and how my faith had developed, since the stories of my unusual events seemed to be faith connected. At that point, I had no idea that the one who needed this explanation was me! And it turned out that I didn't need the explanation to show any connection between my stories and faith. I needed the explanation to help me complete my education about myself and to uncover the roots of my slight depression.

A few weeks into the project it became crystal clear to me that our parents' fights were the roots of the varying degrees of depression my brother and I had throughout life. Just as I was starting to make that connection, I started attending men's group meetings at my church. I went for social reasons, but, interestingly, our course explored in depth the very issues affecting my childhood. As a result of that class (33, The Series, volume 2), connecting the two became a slam dunk instead of a tentative layup!

My need to learn about science, mentioned earlier, was easier to satisfy than was my need to learn about people, including myself. Being the son of my dad – throughout his life, he was almost always reading about science, and he frequently discussed science with my brother and me when we were children – being a physician, and staying current with the publication, *Science News Magazine*, took care of this need. Incidentally, in my first few years of reading *Science News Magazine*, on rare occasion I would think that I might somehow be able to use all of this reading for some grand purpose regarding science. But just as quickly as those thoughts would come I would think "What could I possibly write or say about science that would be of any use to anyone?"

My need to have a strong faith was taken care of by God, Himself. He put me into a family in which having a strong faith wouldn't be a problem at all; my mother was the "Statue of Liberty" of faith!!! And He continued helping the development of my faith by bringing me to my current church, a church whose pastor is extremely inspiring to me.

Lastly, but certainly not least, another need that God took care of Himself was providing me with the unusual events that I have written about. These events constituted the very reason for me to even begin to think about writing. I don't think that He gave me these experiences just for my personal amusement; I am sure that He wanted me to write. And by giving me this writing project, I think that He was also answering, in a delayed manner, part of my "going to work prayer" that I had been praying for at least ten to twelve years before retirement. Specifically, the part that He was answering was the part about helping me to be eager, thankful, and happy to work. This was never answered anywhere near the level that I had hoped for during my medical career, but it was 100% answered with this project!

In the end, God may have directly taken care of all of the various needs that I just sought to explain.

My Best Chance

During a bike ride (of course) it occurred to me that writing this book is probably the best chance that I will ever be given to serve God. I was somewhat aware of this earlier, but it became very clear during that ride. I used to think that "living my faith" at work was my best chance to serve God, but now I think that this may be an even better opportunity. And I don't want to blow it!

We are all called to serve God according to the means that He gave us. I do not have the gift of eloquent and persuasive speech, but He has given me the abilities to think and to write, at least adequately enough for this purpose. Whether this is God's specific plan for me, or not, I don't truly know, but it "feels" like it is!

The gift of inspiration

Throughout my career, I encountered or heard about physicians and other medical professionals who seemed to have a true passion for their work. Their examples were inspirational to me, but would also lead me to think about how I felt about my own medical career. At these times, I would realize that my passion for work was, at most, moderate by comparison, and I was somewhat envious of those with greater work-related passion.

As I have become immersed in this project, however, I am finding that I have inspiration far greater than anything I ever imagined for myself, except, maybe, the inspiration that I had for marrying my wife, and that inspiration was facilitated by the hormones of a young man. With this project, I have found a sustained joy in work that I never have had before. I didn't know that this would become the second biggest adventure of my life (the biggest has been my forty plus years with my wife, along with the fewer years with our sons and their families). I have had countless positive experiences with patients and their families, but the joy of working wasn't sustained, partly because the pace of work usually exceeded my comfort level, and the positive experiences were mixed with many experiences that weren't so positive for the patients and their families.

I can now say that joy and passion for work are possible, and they feel great! Often, I could hardly wait to get back to this project. While writing, often my inspirations would come at such a rate that I felt like a landscape artist, who, while painting a beautiful scene, gets a little frustrated and overwhelmed because new and ever increasingly beautiful hot air balloons keep entering his scene; with each new balloon he thinks, "Yes, I think that I will add you to my painting." And before he is done with that one, another one enters the scene, and so on...

...Sometimes my imagination center must feel like my grandsons as they run around, nonstop! And I love seeing how the words fall into place. I love stretching my mind, then letting it snap back into place, to see which words fall out, where they land, and with what or with whom they have paired. Is their descent slowed by colorful parachutes, or drab ones? Are they lightweights and losers, shattering upon impact, or do they like to give the impression that they are strong, ready to jump up and punch someone in the nose immediately after landing? Or are they truly strong, not feeling threatened by anyone around them, and ready to extend a helping hand?

I never knew that I could get excited about writing, probably because I never had the opportunity to write somewhat creatively on a topic I have become passionate about. And possibly my newfound inspiration is partly due to something else happening.

All of my recent inspiration and joy make me now wonder whether until recently, I have always had some degree of depression. Throughout life I didn't feel sad very often, except when I felt like I was burning out from work, and then, I blamed it on my work demands. But, considering my current levels of joy, inspiration, and peace, and knowing that I never had anything like these feelings before, except for brief occasions, I thought that I should look into this some more. So, for the first time in many years, I looked up the symptoms of depression...with myself in mind for the first time ever. I found that all of the things that have bugged me for most of my life were there on the list. These things included crankiness and irritability, occasional dissatisfaction with various of aspects of my life, lack of assertiveness, lack of inspiration, shyness, periods of low self-esteem, and pickiness. I wasn't affected badly, but just enough to deprive me of a lot of the work-related passion, joy, and job satisfaction that I otherwise might have had.

For a long time, I would occasionally think that I picked the wrong profession, but now I think that I would have been bugged by these same things no matter what type of career I would have chosen. And, in case you were wondering, should I have become a minister? No, I don't think so. I think that I would have been quite uncomfortable in that role. And in that role, I probably wouldn't have learned enough science to be comfortable with writing parts of this book, had I even been inspired to write it.

Looking back, I think that I was able to get through medical school, residency, and my career mostly due to three factors: encouragement from my wife (by her love and presence in my life), academic discipline developed by the time I had reached junior high school, and prayer, which I relied on more heavily in the last fifteen to twenty years of my career. My self-motivation was often inadequate to help me with these tasks.

This project has been what I have needed for a long time, although as I was getting started, I didn't have any idea that I actually needed it. I merely had feelings and poorly defined thoughts as to why I needed to get started. The more I progressed, the sharper my thoughts became. Now I think of this project as having a restorative effect, lifting me up from the slight depression that I never knew I had.

Well, enough of searching through the annals of cause and effect. And, whatever the cause, I like the effect! If Ponce de Leon had only arrived in Florida now, instead of just over 500 years ago, I could have told him about my fountain of youth. My level of inspiration gives me energy and makes me feel young! Oh, Yahoo!

Afterthought

    I have a minor complaint regarding all of my newfound inspiration. I noticed a few weeks ago that I haven't had my favorite dream for quite a while. My "flying dream," as I like to call it, is one that I have had occasionally throughout the better part of my adult life. I have the ability to fly like a bird, although not quite as gracefully as a bird. My arms are used as wings even though they still look like arms. In some episodes of this dream, I've even had a few cool escapes by taking flight. The dream has always been fun, and as you can imagine, and I miss it! I've recently concluded a couple of things about why my dream is no longer occurring. Perhaps it was a gift from God to keep my imagination center in good shape until my slight depression lifted, and it (my imagination center) could take flight on its own. I'm hoping that it had another purpose – to provide me with a preview of sorts. I'm hoping that it was a preview of one of my capabilities in Heaven!

Unusual occurrences

In the introduction, I mentioned five unusual events. The first three are what inspired me to think about writing in the first place; the last two occurred while I was completing this project. For me, these events were not only very interesting (an understatement, of course), but they were also faith strengthening!

5:42

It was April 29, 2011, about 4:30 or 4:40 PM. I was standing at the foot of the bed, looking at my brother, Marvin. I suddenly felt frustrated and impatient, mostly for him but also partly for me........

Marvin was in his third day of hospice care. He had been diagnosed with stage four colon cancer about nineteen months earlier, and had ended treatment for his cancer about three months earlier when it was obvious that the only way for him to win his battle with cancer was to let nature take its course and allow his faith and death to carry him to victory. For the first two days of his hospice care he appeared weak and very ill when awake, but he was still able to speak to us a little. He wanted to get the process of dying over with! His last words to my wife and me, the previous afternoon, were, "I love you guys".

The third day, April 29, was different. Except for a few seconds in the late morning or early afternoon, he was unconscious the entire day. For those few seconds when his eyes were open, he weakly but quickly said a few words. I couldn't understand him, but my wife thought that he had said, "There's a storm coming." He then closed his eyes and never spoke again. His eyes were sunken. His mouth was dry and gaped open. His lips were parched and cracked. He was emaciated. Except for his breathing, he appeared dead. Between 4:00 and 4:30 his hospice nurse arrived to check on him. She didn't think that he would die until the next day.........

I had tried to be patient with his dying process, but I knew that he wanted to get it over with. I had been frequently praying for him, not only for him to die quickly, but also for him to remain strong in his faith. I had been patient until the moment between 4:30 and 4:40 PM, when I was standing at the foot of his bed, looking at him. Then, in an instant, my patience was gone! Instead, I felt frustration and anguish. As I stood there I thought, "I'm going to sit down and ask, 'When will this end?'" I then immediately wondered, "Can I do that?", thinking that this would possibly be disrespectful to God. Instantly, I felt reassurance that, yes, I could indeed do that! All of this took just a few seconds. I then walked to the couch, sat down, then again looked at Marvin. Then, in my thoughts I prayed, "When will this end?!!"

Immediately, I had a new, unexpected thought. The thought was simply, "Five forty-two." It wasn't "Five four two" and it wasn't "Five hundred forty-two." I wondered, "Where did this come from?" I hadn't expected any answer; the prayer had been more rhetorical, out of frustration and anguish, mostly for Marvin, but also partly for me. I was very surprised by the thought "Five forty-two" and continued to ponder what it meant, if anything. It seemed like a specific time to me. I hadn't been trying to predict a time for his death, and no other potential times for his death entered my mind. Earlier I had been thinking, "Will he die tonight? Or tomorrow morning? Or later during the weekend?"

I sat on the couch and thought about this ("Five forty-two") for another ten to fifteen minutes. During that time, I was aware that I no longer felt frustrated or anguished. Those feelings left me when "Five forty-two" entered my mind. I continued to be intrigued with the possibility that this meant something. I then told my wife that something unusual had happened when I thought to myself, "When will this end?" I didn't tell her that this question had been a prayer. I went on to tell her about "Five forty-two" appearing in my mind immediately after I asked the question, "When will this end?" I mentioned that "Five forty-two" almost seemed like a text message. She seemed interested and said that it sounded like a specific time.

We talked a little more about this during the next few minutes. By then it was about 5PM. Marvin looked the same. His breathing was steady and fairly strong. Nothing appeared imminent. I then told my wife, "I'm getting hungry. Do you want to go get something to eat?" Thankfully, she replied, "We're not leaving this room until after 5:42." I was a little surprised by how seriously she took my revelation; she was taking it more seriously than I was. I was skeptical that "Five forty-two" truly meant anything, but I said, "OK."

For the next twenty to thirty minutes we sat there, in Marvin's room, reminiscing. For part of the time we talked about the day that our friend's sister had died. My wife had taken sandwiches to the family while they were awaiting their loved one's passing. When they became hungry, they left her side for a few minutes to prepare their food and start eating. After a few minutes, a family member noticed that their loved one had died (I think that the expression "checked out" was used) while they had stepped away.

At 5:30 PM, I noticed that Marvin's breathing was still the same. I told my wife that it didn't look like he would be going at 5:42. At 5:36, however, his breathing pattern abruptly changed. It became irregular in rhythm and depth.

The irregularity worsened. We moved close to Marvin, wondering, "Could this be happening?" His breathing was definitely consistent with agonal breathing. I grasped Marvin's right hand and occasionally checked his pulse. It was weak. Our eyes kept going back and forth between Marvin and the clock on the wall. It was almost 5:42! A few seconds before 5:42, I noticed that my watch was in sync with the wall clock, to the second; I hadn't noticed that before. Marvin's last inhalation occurred precisely at 5:42:00, by both my watch and the wall clock! At that moment, while holding Marvin's hand, I said, "Goodbye, Marvin."

My wife and I continued to stand by Marvin's bed, in amazement. We weren't at all sad. We were feeling a mixture of happiness for Marvin and absolute awe from something very unusual having happened. We soon sat down, but our combination of happiness and amazement continued as we thought, and occasionally talked, about what had just happened. We didn't even think to call the nurse to inform her. She walked in a few minutes later and we told her what had just happened. She was probably thinking, "What is wrong with these people? Why didn't they call me right away?" She checked Marvin and said that she needed to call the doctor to pronounce him dead. It took a few more minutes for the doctor to arrive and do his duty. Officially, Marvin's time of death was much closer to 6 PM, but we, and now you, know the true time of his death.

I have thought about "5:42" every day since then. On November 14, 2015, my wife and I were attending my aunt's funeral. During a conversation with my cousin about Marvin, the story of his death and "5:42" came up. That was the first time I had told anyone that 5:42 was the answer to a prayer.

My prayer that was answered with the thought "5:42" was not a usual prayer for me. I don't think that I had ever prayed that way before, but nonetheless, I still regarded it as a prayer. This became clearer to me in the Spring of 2015 when I was reading our weekly church bulletin in which our pastor had written about different types of prayer. When I got to the part about "prayer of complaint," I thought, "That's it! '5:42' was the answer to a prayer of complaint!"

As you will become aware, I have been praying for a relatively long time, but I don't think that I had ever before offered a prayer of complaint to God, and I haven't offered one since then, either. And I don't think that I had ever before prayed with the anguish and frustration that I felt when I prayed, "When will this end?" (Incidentally, I also think that at least a second prayer was answered that day. Just before I prayed, "When will this end?", I had questioned "Can I do that?" I think the immediate reassurance I felt after that thought was also the answer to a prayer).

I have told a few other people about "5:42". After telling the story to one of my partners in the ER, she said, "God spoke to you!" I replied, "Either He, or someone working for Him did."

In 2014, while reading the Bible, I had a moment of enlightenment about "5:42". John 16:13 says, "Howbeit when he, the Spirit of truth, is come, he will guide you into all truth: for he shall not speak of himself; but whatsoever he shall hear, that shall he speak, and he will shew (show) you things to come." When I read this, it was an "Aha" moment. I believe that "5:42" was conveyed to my consciousness by the Holy Spirit (the Spirit of truth). I continue to be awed by this!

I have often thought about "5:42" in terms of what it tells me about God. I think the answer ("5:42") that He gave me may possibly be showing a happy, fun-loving side of

God. You might ask, "Why is that? How can that be?" Well, I think that God might have been giving me some good-natured kidding when He gave me that answer. You see, "5:42", or something like it, is often how I have answered questions that can be answered by a number. When a question calls for an approximate numeric answer, I have often answered with unnecessarily precise sounding numbers, such as, "I'm 83% sure," or "It broke into 874 pieces." This has been my tendency since junior high, when I had a need to feel "cool." It was then that I learned about the laughter that our science teacher had provoked when he told Marvin's class about his child dropping and breaking something that had been meaningful to him. He had said that it broke into 937 pieces (or something like that). It didn't seem that he was trying to be funny. His delivery of the story was in a serious tone, but the unnecessarily precise sounding number in his story provoked laughter. That seemed "cool" to me.....And God may have been telling me that His precise sounding numbers are exactly that (precise), whereas mine have never been.

You might ask, "Why would God do this at such a solemn occasion as death?" Maybe He was telling me (and now you) that death is not necessarily a solemn, sad occasion, but rather, that it can be a happy, joyous occasion. For my wife and me, "5:42" was happy and joyous. It was happy and joyous especially because Marvin was breaking free from the misery of his cancer and from his private wasteland of depression. He was entering a realm in which he could be always laughing, always happy! Oh, Yahoo!

The Seizure

Our granddaughter experienced a seizure when she was a toddler. She and her parents were living in Moscow,

Russia, at the time. Her seizure was treated en route to the hospital. The rescue squad included a physician. Thankfully, she did well, and hasn't had more seizures. It sounded like she received great medical care, and the care was very affordable. I am thankful for her good outcome and for the great care that she received.

But what you just read is not why I am writing about her seizure. I am including the story of her seizure because I had an unusual part in that story. I suspect that not very many grandparents have had such connections to their grandchildren's health issues.

I did not tell our son and daughter-in-law (and granddaughter) the story of my connection to our granddaughter's seizure until I wrote the family version of this book. I had told my wife about this immediately after we learned about her seizure, but we decided not to tell our son and daughter-in-law since we both thought that it would be upsetting to them. But I always thought that I would eventually tell them, and "eventually" arrived with the first version of this book.

Our son had called us about an hour before the seizure occurred. He first talked to his mom, then to me. During my conversation with him, his daughter was near him and he was trying to get her to say something for me. As you know, getting a toddler to speak on request is difficult. I was listening intently. She then said something, although I couldn't discern what it was that she said. At the exact instant that I heard her, I experienced a very brief but very vivid mental image of her face; the image lasted probably less than a second. In this image, the left side of her face was clearly twitching with seizure activity. Understandably, that briefly stunned me. I didn't know what to make of it. Of course, she was fine at that time. I didn't say anything about this to our son or my wife at the time because it didn't make sense to me and I didn't see any point in telling either of them.

We finished the phone call a short time later. Our son then called us about an hour later to tell us that his daughter was having a problem. What he described to me was seizure activity. I told him to call the Moscow equivalent of 911. He had already called them. He gave us a further update a little later. As you already know, she did well.

When he had initially called back to report on his daughter's seizure, I was doubly stunned; foremost, about her seizure, and secondly, about my "preview" of the episode. After this second call, I told my wife about my "preview" experience.

I replayed this experience in my mind many times after her seizure, but the frequency became less and less – until we experienced "5:42." As you can imagine, the thoughts I had of my "preview" of our granddaughter's seizure began to come back more frequently, for it reminded me of "5:42." Both were forms of advance knowledge, and both were received by me about an hour before the actual event. Although my daily prayer of course included my granddaughter, my "preview" of her seizure was not an obvious answer to a prayer like "5:42" had been.

I will return to our granddaughter's seizure and "5:42" after the following story.

Miracle?

This story took place in the early 1990s when I was working a day shift in the ER. I was sitting in the office when a nurse (whom I will call RN) came to tell me that I was needed. She described a pale, unresponsive child as I walked with her to the exam room. I clearly recall feeling calm and confident that the child would be okay, even from the moment that RN had started telling me about the child. In fact, my first thought when RN started telling me about our patient was, "Why is she so upset? The child is going to do well." Of course, I didn't tell her this thought.

When I entered the exam room I could see that the child, a little girl, was lying on the exam bed, motionless except for her breathing. I don't remember her age, but I think that she was somewhere between one and three years old. She was pale. Her eyes were closed. As I listened to her heart and lungs with my stethoscope, she remained pale and motionless. I then started to examine her abdomen by palpation (examination by hand). Her abdomen seemed okay, but within a second or two after I touched her abdomen, she opened her eyes and started to regain normal color. Within another few seconds her color was normal and she sat up and started looking around. She started interacting with her mother. She seemed normal at that point.

RN, who had been very concerned about the child, looked at me and said, "It's a miracle!" I was surprised by her pronouncement, but didn't take her very seriously; I wasn't sure that she was serious. I figured that the child was about to improve and wake up anyway, and that it was just a coincidence that her quick improvement was simultaneous with my hands first touching her (when I had examined her chest, only my stethoscope, and not my hands, had touched her chest). I do not remember much of the history of her illness. I think that she had briefly been ill, and had worsened before her mother brought her to the ER. By the time she arrived at the ER, she was pale and unresponsive. I don't recall any mention of seizure-like activity, and I don't recall if she had fever or vomiting. I would probably be able to recall more details of her history had I taken RN's pronouncement more seriously at that time.

Because the girl improved so quickly after I started examining her, I wasn't very worried about her. But because of her pallor and unresponsiveness, I decided to have blood tests done and observe her for a while longer. Her test results were good and she continued to do well. She interacted normally and ate and drank. Apart from her first minute or two in the ER, she appeared to be a normal, well child. I don't remember what diagnosis I put on her chart. I never heard any additional feedback on her, so I assume that she continued to do well. Normally, I would have been informed if she had returned to the ER or had been admitted to the hospital.

In subsequent years, I would think about this child's case, on occasion, mainly in regard to RN stating, "It's a miracle!" For years, I didn't regard it as a miracle. However, since we experienced "5:42", I haven't been so sure.

In recent months, these events ("5:42", our granddaughter's seizure, and the child's case that I just described) have been on my mind a lot. Regarding the child's case, two things stand out in my mind as being unusual. The first was my combined sense of calmness and confidence (confidence that the child would do well), even before I saw her, despite RN's significant concern. RN was not inexperienced; she was an experienced and very good pediatric emergency nurse. Normally, I would have felt some degree of unease while walking to the exam room in a situation like this. This time there was none. As we walked to the child's exam room, RN may have been wondering why I didn't seem more concerned. I don't recall ever having had the same complete sense of calmness and confidence in dealing with a potentially serious illness in a child, especially before seeing the child.

The second unusual thing was this child's instantaneous, or almost instantaneous, improvement when I touched her for the first time. Occasionally in the years following this child's case, I jokingly referred to it as my case of "laying on of the hands," similar to miracles described in the Bible. But I didn't truly think that it was a miracle. Now, however, my opinion has changed. While I don't know for certain whether it was a miracle, I think that it was more likely than not.

My feeling of calmness and confidence that I experienced with this child was not the result of any conscious decision beforehand. It was just "there," without any effort or forethought on my part whatsoever.

If this child's case truly was a miracle, I have an idea of how it played out. The mother, other family members, friends, or RN were praying with great faith for this child. God decided to answer the prayer in the manner I have described. He saw fit to accomplish the miracle by involving me to convey His healing power to the child in the form of a healing touch. My sense of calmness and confidence, with absolutely no doubt in my mind about a good outcome forthcoming for the child, was part of the process of Him involving me. And this was done so subtly by Him that I didn't question it at the time.

I will probably never know with complete certainty, at least in this present world, if this truly was a miracle. While I now think that it was a miracle more likely than not, it might have simply been a couple of odd coincidences associated with a child who was going to do well anyway. But even the thought that it might have been a miracle is awe-inspiring to me!

I have further thoughts on "5:42" and our granddaughter's seizure. I think that with these episodes,

God was saying something like, "I'm here, I care about you, and I am aware of what is going on with you and your family." And I do not think that God caused our granddaughter's seizure, or that he caused Marvin to die at 5:42 PM. I believe that He has always known that she would have a seizure and that he conveyed the "preview" to me via the Holy Spirit, just like He conveyed to me the exact time of Marvin's death, which He also has always known.

These unusual events are on my mind every day. With them, I feel that I have had the privilege or gift of brief personal glimpses of the amazing power and love of God! I am awed by many aspects of God and His relationship with us; in these instances, I am awed especially by the ways in which God chooses to interact with us!

Recently, I read another Bible verse that might possibly explain why I have had these unusual experiences. James 4:8 says, "Draw nigh to God and He will draw nigh to you." I also have another thought that was already presented in "How did this occur? Was it God's plan, or simply mine?

Musical "Reverie"

It was November 1, 2015 – All Saints Day. The weather was glorious. I was just starting out on a bike ride, but I lingered near our church (we live across the street from our church) because I wanted to hear all of the bells concert that had just started early that afternoon. I'm fairly certain that the first hymn was "A Mighty Fortress is our God," although it might have been, "The Church's One Foundation." At any rate, it sounded great.

Without missing a beat after the first hymn ended, I started "hearing" the first part of "Crown Him with Many

Crowns." I quickly realized that my ears weren't "hearing" the first few measures because there was a pause between hymns. Never before had I so effortlessly sensed music, with or without my ears being involved! And it "sounded" great! My "music" stopped before the actual next (second) hymn started. I had just enough time to wonder what the next hymn would actually be. I expected that it would be what I had just "heard" so clearly in my mind. Sure enough, the next hymn was "Crown Him with Many Crowns", and it started from the beginning, just like it had done earlier in my mind. And, this time, my ears were definitely involved. I don't remember what the third hymn was, probably because I was thinking so much about the short "preview" (or "pre-listen") that I had just experienced.

Now, I will always have an All Saints Day memory.

3 AM Awakening

This occurred around January 11-12, 2016. I had woken up abruptly, more startled than frightened, with a Bible verse seared strongly in my thoughts! I was also aware that I had a faster pulse than usual and faster and deeper breathing than usual. I was simultaneously conscious of the Bible verse as I awakened. I have no recollection of dreaming just before being startled awake. The Bible verse imprinted in my mind was, "Go ye therefore and teach all nations, baptizing them in the name of the Father, and of the Son, and of the Holy Spirit." This is Matthew 28:19.

Never before had I experienced anything like this while awakening, abruptly or otherwise. I have a very strong feeling that this Bible verse being imprinted in my thoughts simultaneously with my startling 3 AM awakening is more than the random workings of my mind. That said, I can't prove any of this to anyone who requires more definite proof. In fact, very little that I write here can be proven by our earthly standards.

Afterthoughts

Pertinent to our discussion at the moment, I once told the story of my 3 AM Awakening to my friends in my Tuesday evening men's group at church. Incidentally, several of these men have knowledge of the Bible that runs circles around mine. As I finished my story, I added that I thought my 3 AM Awakening was caused by the Holy Spirit. My friend noted for the most fastidious study and knowledge of the Bible within our group disagreed with my last statement. He said something like the following, "Our inspiration from the Holy Spirit is gentler than what you describe. Your awakening was most likely caused by Jesus, Himself!".......As I periodically think of my friend's interpretation, I have three main thoughts: 1) "After all, those were the words of Jesus." 2) "Who am I to disagree, since I'm not an expert on this." And 3) "Cool!"

Further Thoughts

I think that God probably interacts with people in each generation in a manner similar to what I have experienced. God could certainly interact with us more strongly, more definitely, and in a more widespread manner than He does, if He so chose. This would remove any doubt about His existence and His power and love. But He doesn't do this, although the reasons are likely beyond my understanding. I do think that in our current sinful state it would be far too overwhelming for us to experience God in bigger doses. Not only that, but it would interfere with the Free Will that He has given us (I believe that it is up to us to either embrace God or to deny Him). And it might actually interfere with our faith development. If God were obvious to us, we wouldn't need to develop our faith. God highly values our faith in Him, since it is a form of love. But God gives some of us more definite glimpses of His existence, power, and love to inspire and reinforce our faith in Him. He does this both for our own needs and for the needs of those with whom we share this information.

Near misses (x6)

I have experienced at least six near miss situations in my life. One of these I shared with my wife, one I shared with Marvin, and one I shared with a classmate who was both a relative and friend. The other three were solo events. These were situations in which I, or we, could have easily been seriously injured or even killed. By the fifth experience, occurring in 1990, I started to wonder, "Is this just dumb luck, or is someone praying very hard for me, or am I being kept around (on earth) for a specific purpose?"

"Is this what dying is like?"

I was about 11 or 12 years old. It was summertime. I was with my family during a fishing outing a few miles north of North Loup, Nebraska. As usual, my mom was fishing and my dad was sitting on a lawn chair and reading (probably Popular Science). Marvin and I were climbing a tree. Everything was going well until I heard a crack and felt movement that I hadn't intentionally initiated. I had been sitting on a branch, twenty feet above the ground, and about five to seven feet out from where the branch connected to the trunk. Before I could try to do anything to avert disaster, I was falling! Thud!!! I was on my back. I was dazed and was seeing stars, but I do remember an awful feeling of needing to get air into my lungs, and quickly! My thought at the time was, "Is this what dying is like?" I remember seeing my dad running to me (I don't ever remember seeing him so excited and concerned as he was then), and by the time he got to me, I was starting to take breaths. I felt much better. Dad did his "medical screening exam." My back and chest had hurt initially, but that pain subsided in less than a minute. I had no pain elsewhere, including my head, neck, abdomen, and extremities. I quickly became fully alert, my breathing was normal, I moved my neck and extremities normally, and then I stood up and walked without difficulty. Fortunately, I had landed on my back in a grassy area. Had I landed on my head, I probably would have fractured my neck, and you probably wouldn't be reading this, either!

Not a Sweet Ride

I was in the seventh grade. It was about 4:30 PM, on a late fall or early winter day. I had volunteered to ride our horse, Sugar, to check on the cattle in the fields. I put on her bridle, led her to the manger, then mounted her while standing on the manger. I hadn't put on the saddle. I usually didn't use the saddle because I enjoyed riding bareback, and besides, it takes extra time to put on a saddle.

I rode out into the fields. Nothing was amiss. I decided to extend the ride by going around the perimeter of our farm. Then something, unknown to me, spooked Sugar. She bucked while in a trot, which led to me flying up into the air above her. I landed on the side of her neck as she was suddenly accelerating into a full gallop. I was able to grasp her mane and wrap my arms around her neck while hanging on from under her neck. She continued galloping at full speed for a quarter of a mile while I hung on. I think that it was my adrenaline release that gave me the needed strength to gradually pull myself, using my arms and legs, back up onto her back. It took most of the quarter mile to get back up where I should have been. I didn't want to let go and just fall to the ground because I was fairly certain that one or more of her hooves would trample me. Once I had regained a proper riding position, I was able to get her stopped. The rest of the ride was uneventful.

To the Cemetery

While in high school I asked RF (my classmate, who was a Relative and Friend) if I could ride with him to the Memorial Day observance at the North Loup cemetery. We were in neighboring Scotia, Nebraska at the high school. We were both in band and we were going to play for the observance. I think that we were the last to leave from the band room for the cemetery, and it looked like we would be late (not a surprise to some of you who know me, I suspect). I suggested going on back roads (less likelihood of getting caught for speeding). RF took the gravel road that was on the edge of our farm. Soon we were going 90 mph. Probably a little later than I should have, I reminded RF of a dip in the road (the dip had been constructed for water drainage over the road during rainstorms as an alternative to placing a culvert below the road). There was an accumulation of loose gravel in the dip, which, combined with his braking, led to RF losing his ability to keep the car on the road. We entered the ditch and climbed up onto the embankment on the other side of the ditch. It looked like we were going to crash into a large tree in the fence line of our farm, but luckily RF avoided the tree. He was able to get the car back through the ditch and onto the road before stopping about 40 to 50 yards beyond the tree. When he stopped the car, we both looked at each other with relief on our faces. We both got out of the car when RF said that he wanted to see how close his car had come to the tree. We found that the smashed grass from the wheels was about five to six inches from the tree! He had probably been able to slow the car to about 60 to 70 mph as we had passed the tree. We both realized that we had narrowly avoided disaster! The rest of the way to the cemetery he sped more sensibly, probably 70–75 mph. We were there just in time for the performance, but I think we may have had to jog from the car, carrying our instruments. Incidentally, during our experience, we weren't wearing seat belts; I can't remember if RF's car even had seat belts.

Shaken, and Slightly Stirred

This near miss occurred just before I started my sophomore year of college. Marvin and I were driving through the Snake River Valley in northern Nebraska to Merritt Reservoir. We were going to camp for one night, which we ultimately did, but not until after a little unplanned excitement.

I was driving. I became briefly distracted (also probably not a surprise) by the scenery. There were some scenic areas in the part of Nebraska where we grew up, but nothing to match the Snake River Valley. Even then I had an appreciation for the beauty of God's creation. My distraction by the scenery coincided with a curve in the road. It only took about a second before I realized that driving required my full attention, but by then, the wheels on the passenger side were on the shoulder. I overcorrected, and this immediately led to cycles of the car rocking from side to side, on two wheels at a time. We were going about 55–60 mph. I think that there were about six or more cycles of rocking before I was able to regain proper control of the car. I then stopped the car on the side of the road. The car seemed fine and we were okay except for being a little shaken and slightly stirred. Amazingly, it seemed at first, Marvin didn't object to me continuing to drive, but looking back I suspect that he was reassured by the thought that I would give my full attention to driving from that point on. The rest of the trip went according to plan.

That car did have lap belts, incidentally, and it's possible we were even wearing them during the episode that I just described.

Safe Arrival at Church

In 1990, shortly after we had moved to Omaha, I was driving back to Fremont to play my trumpet during a church service. I was to play during two of the hymns. The previous year there had been a request for a volunteer to play the trumpet at church. I said that if there were no other volunteers, I could do it, but I would need a few weeks to practice and get to a reasonable level, although I'm quite certain that I set the expectation that my playing wouldn't be "any great shakes." I hadn't played any instrument since January 1, 1973, and hadn't played a trumpet, or cornet, since the seventh or eighth grade.

The road was icy. Traffic was moving very slowly, between 25 and 30 mph. Beyond the town of Valley I encountered a particularly icy spot. Some of the cars ahead of me were sliding into the ditch. As a semi-truck approached from the other direction, I found that I could no longer control my Ford Bronco II; it started sliding across the road into the lane with oncoming traffic. Even though we were driving just under half the speed limit, the semi-truck and my vehicle seemed to be speeding towards certain impact. It was happening so fast that I didn't even get to the point of praying or swearing. Fortunately, my vehicle completed its slide across the lane and entered the ditch on that side just as the semi was within about 5–8 feet of impact (I had full view of the oncoming semi the entire time until it passed). The snow and grass in the ditch provided better traction and I immediately regained control. I was able to keep driving in the ditch for about a hundred yards, without any stop or interruption, until it appeared safe to pull back onto the road and cross into the proper lane.

Looking back at this episode, my driving in the ditch and back onto the road without any difficulty went so smoothly that it seemed like a well-executed, planned maneuver. The other drivers nearby may have been watching my vehicle with incredulity similar to that of the people on the beach watching James Bond drive his car out of the sea in The Spy Who Loved Me (I have always liked Bond movies).

There were no further close calls during the trip, and I arrived safely at church. And probably not surprisingly, my level of thankfulness was greater than usual during the church service!

Incidentally, you have already read about one of the hymns that I played during that service (see Musical Reverie). It was Crown Him With Many Crowns. This didn't occur to me until I started typing the story of this episode. Since I have "come full circle" with that hymn, I now feel a special connection with it. I probably should learn its words.

Mayhem

My wife and I shared this experience in 2013. We were taking a fall drive to Auburn and Nebraska City. The weather was gorgeous. The fall color was good by the standards of western Iowa and eastern Nebraska, but poor by those of the eastern US. After leaving Nebraska City on the return trip we drove on a two-lane highway, with the speed limit being 65 mph; I was driving the speed limit. It was a routine drive until suddenly a small yellow car left the lane of oncoming traffic and entered our lane; that car also appeared to be traveling at the speed limit. My wife could see that the driver was looking down, probably texting. I think that I was briefly able to honk as I jerked the steering wheel to the right. Instantly there was a loud noise from impact with the oncoming car. I was able to stop fairly quickly on the shoulder on our side of the road. We saw the other car, driven by Mayhem, as we're fond of calling its driver, speeding away in the correct lane. Because of the loud impact noise, we expected to see some damage on the driver's side of my car. The side mirror was broken and part of it was dangling, but there was not so much as a scratch anywhere else on the car.

Apparently, our cars had passed each other in parallel, probably about four to six inches apart. Our cars were close enough for the mirrors to crash together, but nothing beyond that. It seems that Mayhem must have jerked his car to his right at just the right time and just enough to avoid an impact involving more than side mirrors.

We stood on the roadside for a couple of minutes, regaining our composures, then continued the drive home.

I was so thankful that we were able to avoid injury, or worse, that I didn't give a second thought to paying nearly $500 for a new mirror.

Another detail of this story, one that I didn't tell my wife about until very recently, was that I was saying my daily prayer at the time that Mayhem struck.

Inspired by a movie

My wife and I went to a movie today (March 10, 2016). It was her suggestion. I was skeptical of her choice, but I agreed. She wanted to see *Spotlight*. It was a great movie, and I shouldn't have been skeptical about going to see it, but I'm not writing this to sing the praises of the movie. As you may know, the movie tells the story of investigative journalists uncovering the crimes of child and adolescent sexual abuse committed by Roman Catholic priests in and around Boston and the cover-up of those crimes by the priests' superiors. These crimes and the associated cover-up needed to be exposed.

While driving back home after the movie I was thinking about how terrible these crimes were. And they were committed by people we trust to be good examples for all of us. I then thought about how we are all sinners, and all of us have fallen short of the glory of God, which gradually led me to think about forgiveness for the priests. For many people, these crimes are unforgivable. I suspect that some of the victims have forgiven their abusers and that others never will. But will God forgive these crimes of abuse by the priests? Another question to consider is that even if these priests are properly penitent for God to forgive them, will they be able to forgive themselves?

I believe that God can forgive these crimes if those who commit them are indeed penitent and ask Him for forgiveness. I believe that it is harder for people to forgive these priests than for God to forgive them. I think that all sins are forgivable by God except unbelief in Him (God the Father, God the Son, and God the Holy Spirit). The ability of all sins to be forgiven is difficult for most people to accept, including me sometimes, but I think that this is what our Triune God has taught us. In regard to forgiveness for the priests, I like to think of the Apostle Paul (known as Saul of Tarsus before his conversion). Before his conversion to Christianity, accomplished directly by Jesus, he oversaw, or at least was complicit in the deaths and torture of many Christians. He was in support of the removal of Christians. He was certain that he was doing the right thing for God and for Judaism. After his conversion, he found great zeal for spreading the good news about Jesus, the Son of God the Father. I think that if Paul could be forgiven and put to such good use in God's kingdom, the priests in question can also be forgiven.

Even if the priests can be forgiven by God and by some of us, can they return to their previous calling?......No! Only God would know which ones are completely rehabilitated and trustworthy. Further abuse needs to be prevented, and we wouldn't know which of the priests, if any, could be trusted to lead a parish or to be alone with children and adolescents. I do believe that there should be some capacity in which they could continue to serve God, but safeguards would be required to prevent further abuse.

And even if these priests are properly penitent and otherwise able to serve God in some capacity, would they be able to forgive themselves enough to be able to do any effective service? This question is related to something that I learned from our pastor. That is, the tendency to continually "beat ourselves up" about certain sins and inability to forgive ourselves even though we are properly penitent for these sins is a "gift" from Satan. In other words, Satan wants to interfere with us being able to feel forgiven by God. He wants to deprive us of the restoration that we receive with forgiveness. If we appear to be on the right track (from God's point of view), Satan wants to give us a dose of desperation and doubt about our worthiness. He will do anything that he can to undermine and weaken our faith.

In closing, I think that we should pray this prayer, as needed, "Lord, please help me to be able to forgive myself when I know that I have forgiveness from You." What is in the past we can't change, but, when we are forgiven, we have a new start and we can be very hopeful of doing better in the future!

There was one more indirect inspiration for me from the movie. On the way home I asked my wife what she thought was the reason for Robbie balking on the release of the story. I asked, "Do you think that it was because he felt bad for not adequately following up on his leads from 20 years earlier?" I think that she hit the nail on the head when she said, "He had already missed on one chance to get the story right. Now that he had a second chance, he wanted to be absolutely sure that it was right before it was released." What a good answer! Then I thought, "This could apply to me and my writing. Late last fall I tried to rush through this project in order to get it done by Thanksgiving, but then I found that I wasn't happy with the results. I gave myself a second chance to 'get it right'."

My secret mentor

Jim was my mentor. He didn't know it, at least I don't think he did. Actually, I didn't know it either until one day late in the fall of 2015 when I was thinking about him. But looking back, it turns out that I felt it long before I knew it in my conscious thoughts.

About thirty years my senior, Jim was one of the kindest, wisest, and most thoughtful men I have ever known. His wonderful blend of quiet confidence, quiet pride, and humility was truly inspirational. And despite his elderly voice, I always found him so eloquent.

We met when he and his dear wife Andree moved into our condo building. I became especially interested in him when I heard through my wife that Andree thought of him as a spiritual man. From that point on I longed to talk to him about some of the things that I am now writing about in this book. But it never happened! We never got to that point in our visits or conversations. And our move, followed by his death about five months later, ensured that we'd never get to that point, at least not in this world!

I have imagined Jim bearing some responsibility for my recent "self-enlightenment", and for my ability to find peace. I have the feeling that he liked me, and I sense that in his wisdom he may have noticed something that prompted him to offer a prayer like the following: "God, could you please help Alan? I'm not sure that he will be truly be at peace, even with retirement. He needs just a little inspirational nudge so that he can know himself better. I think that he can be pretty happy if You do that for him."

Thanks, Jim! 'til we meet again!

Getting excited about a trip

If you are like me, you tend to get excited about an upcoming trip. I think that I have always been that way. In recent years, I have had the habit of making a list of what I want to pack. I will occasionally calculate how many days there are until our departure. There are times when I have to find distracting activities so that I am not wishing for a faster passage of time while awaiting the trip.

Now I'm planning for a bigger trip than I've ever taken before. The travel brochure is the biggest one that I've ever seen. The first time I looked at the brochure I paged through it, looking for pictures. I was disappointed that there were no pictures! Since then, though, I have periodically read various parts of the brochure. I have found that the writers of the brochure were confident enough in their ability to arrange words that they didn't need to include pictures (to them, a thousand words are worth a picture, or something like that). At various points, they describe my new destination in glowing terms.....paradise, many mansions, streets lined with precious metals, gems and pearls used in various structures, etc. (I've always liked to tour mansions, and I think that I will be okay with gold and gems too).

I've looked in the brochure for recommendations on what type of clothing to pack, but, as far as I can tell, I don't have to pack anything. It seems that they will provide everything that I need on this upcoming trip. Sounds good to me!

I've researched the cost of the trip. More great news! Apparently, some generous guy already paid for my ticket. In fact, my ticket was included in the brochure. It had strange instructions printed on the back of it. The instructions were: "Do not lose this ticket! It may be difficult to issue you a replacement ticket before your departure date. So hang on to this ticket!" I must not lose my ticket!

I've checked for my departure date, but I can't find it on my ticket. The travel planners apparently don't think that it is important for me to know my departure date. They keep the departure schedule in their office, but they aren't interested in disclosing my date of travel to me. But, to their credit, they will make up for this lack of disclosure. They will do this by sending either a flight attendant, or even the captain himself, to pick me up from my home, or wherever I am, on the date of departure. They say that the trip is more interesting when it comes as a surprise; and they say it will be a good surprise. Sometimes they surprise the travelers with flowers when they pick us up (sort of like the Publisher's Clearing House Prize Patrol, I believe). I guess I can accept a surprise departure. After all, I don't have to pack anything. Apparently, if I'm on one of the more routine, earlier trips, the ones that aren't too packed, it will be a shuttle flight attendant who picks me up and takes me to the shuttle. But if it turns out that I'm not scheduled until the last trip, the captain himself comes to pick me up. And it seems that they must be running a special for the last trip, because I've heard that lots of people will be going on that trip. Obviously, the captain will be very busy that day if he is responsible for picking up all of the passengers. I hope he can work miracles! It certainly seems that he will need to be able to!

I usually don't check this detail for myself, but in case anyone happens to travel with me and wants to know, my destination is not on the list of places that the State Department recommends against traveling to because of increased risk of terrorist activities. It seems that my destination is a very safe place.

There was one other detail to take care of. I like to

shower before taking a trip...sort of like the advice we get from our moms to wear clean underwear in case we are involved in an accident and have to go to the hospital. Anyway, I was a little concerned that with my departure date being a surprise, I might not have time to shower. But, after a little more research of the brochure, it appears that they also took care of this detail. The brochure says that they have some new-fangled cleansing process that all of the passengers receive before boarding. I don't remember all the technical details of this process, but I think that they said that we wouldn't even have to get undressed for it. Wow! It sounds pretty thorough, and even a little miraculous! So, even if I'm hot and sweaty from a bike ride, or even if I have dirty hands from raking leaves and bagging them on the church lot across the street just before I am picked up, I won't have to worry about not being able to shower. Wow! What planners!

Remember me telling you about a generous guy who paid for our tickets? Well, when I checked the brochure recently, I actually found where it says that the captain himself pays for our tickets. Sounds like a really great guy! Hmm, I wonder what's in it for him. I guess I'll have to check the brochure again for that answer. The brochure is so big that it probably has the answer somewhere. Maybe he is just a people-lover.

Well that about does it, except for one thing, hanging on to that ticket! I've been doing some special mental exercises so that I never misplace the ticket. I'm pretty sure I will be all set.

I'm usually not pushy about where others should travel, but my upcoming trip and destination sound so great that I have to be a little pushy; everyone should be seriously looking into taking this trip. I think that anyone who opts not to take this trip with me will really be missing the boat, er, I mean, shuttle.

Belief and Prayer

Bold proclamation!

It's true, folks! It is true!!!!

What's true? This book?

I wasn't referring to this book. (I would like to think that this book is completely true. I know that at least parts of it are true. I tried my best to make sure that the important parts are completely true, but since a lot of it consists of my opinions, and since I am human, I can't be entirely sure. And, of course, my attempts at humor, or more serious fiction, to help make various points, aren't completely true). But the truth I am sure of is God's plan for salvation that is recorded in the New Testament! We receive eternal life with God if we believe that the Son of God, Jesus Christ, paid the price for our salvation!

How do I know this?

This is the faith that I was given as a child, a faith that I have held onto firmly since childhood. I have been blessed with this faith growing ever stronger. And here is the proof that my faith (the faith that was taught to us by Jesus) is the true faith: God has blessed me with brief communications and interactions with Him on several occasions. I am certain that He would not have done so if the faith with which I have been blessed were not the true faith!!!

The purpose of worshipping God

For years, I have intermittently thought about this question: "Why do we worship God?" And not because I don't want to worship God. I enjoy worshipping God!

Does God need our worship? He is a big, powerful God, after all. What would worship of Him by puny creatures, like us, do for Him?

Over the years, as my thoughts focused more and more on the loving qualities of God, I came to the following conclusion (or was blessed with this conclusion): God does not need worship so much as we have a need to worship Him! God wants our companionship, but I do not think that He needs us to grovel in His presence. I do think, however, that in our relationship with Him, we must have the utmost respect for Him and love of Him.

Why do we need to worship Him, when all God desires is simply our companionship? To answer this I, go to two ideas. He created us and understands how we "work". And He gave us free will. Free will implies that we live in an "equal opportunity" world in regard to good and evil. It is up to us to choose our path. The point about God understanding how we "work" comes into play as follows: even though He gave us free will, He knows that we are easily influenced by forces stronger than ourselves. So, if we aren't filling our minds with thoughts about the love, goodness, and power of God, then Satan is more than happy to assist us by providing us with thoughts that lead us in the opposite direction. Worshipping God helps remove some of Satan's opportunities. And if we have a great worship experience, there is more of a worship afterglow that continues to protect us from Satan's ideas. And we can further prolong and enhance our protection from Satan with daily prayer, contemplation of God, and Bible readings.

Judeo-Christianity

FYI: this is not entirely "politically correct", but I don't think that religion is meant to be politically correct.

Before I go any further, I must, as a Christian, express my utter shame for what people of my faith have done to the people of Judaism. And the man who provided the basis of my early Christian instruction, and from whom I still draw inspiration, undoubtedly inspired, or helped inspire the greatest harm to the people of Judaism. This man was Martin Luther. Even though he did great good for Christianity, some of his writings, specifically the ones that were abhorrently anti-Semitic, provided great inspiration to the Third Reich! And no doubt they inspired countless pogroms before the Holocaust. With these writings, he was not acting as a follower of Jesus, but was instead acting as a follower of Satan. I know that not all Christians feel this way, but we should!

Another point regarding the relationship between Christianity and Judaism has been on my mind for a long time, which is that some Christians are upset that the Jews killed Jesus, or, at least that they played such a major role in His death. Feeling this way means that we absolutely do not understand this part of our faith. That the Jews played a huge role in Jesus' death should not be a cause for anger; rather, it should be a cause for celebration and happiness. His (Jesus') suffering and death were absolutely necessary for us, because they, along with His resurrection, provide us the means for our salvation. Therefore, we should Rejoice! both in His death and the role played by the Jews in bringing it about!

Although my faith is called Christianity, often I like to think of it as Judeo-Christianity. (I think that if we Christians embraced more of Judaism, while not letting go of our faith in

Jesus, it would add a richness to our faith that would help us understand it better). I don't remember when and where I first heard the term Judeo-Christian, but I was immediately intrigued by this combined name. It is a name that reflects the long history of my faith. Some would say that my faith wasn't "born" until the last few years of Jesus' life, not quite 2,000 years ago. I would say that my faith is much older than that. Some say it dates back to the time of Adam and Eve, with the following Bible verse being the first reference to Jesus in the Old Testament (Genesis 3:15, "And I will put enmity between thee and the woman, and between thy seed and her seed; it shall bruise thy head, and thou shalt bruise his heel."). I like to think that my faith is even older than that; I think that it dates back to the beginning of the creation, when God, because He was able to know everything in the future, conceived His plan for man's salvation.

The Old Testament contains many prophecies regarding the first appearance of Jesus on earth. One of the best known is Isaiah 9:6, which states, "For unto us a child is born, unto us a son is given: and the government shall be upon his shoulder: and his name shall be called Wonderful, Counsellor, The mighty God, The everlasting Father, The Prince of Peace." In Psalm 22, David speaks very clearly about the crucifixion of Jesus (hundreds of years before the practice of crucifixion started; it was unknown at the time that David lived). One website lists 353 Old Testament prophecies of Jesus. Obviously, the Old Testament is extremely important to Christianity (or Judeo-Christianity).

Of course, most Christians are more familiar with the New Testament than the Old Testament. The stories of Jesus' human existence are told in the New Testament. It also contains His lessons and His examples of how we should live, but, most importantly, it contains what we can simply call "the words of eternal life."

Both the Old Testament and the New Testament are very important to me. I like to think of the Old Testament (and Judaism) as the foundation (as in the foundation of my faith), and I like to think of the New Testament (and Christianity) as the fulfillment (the fulfillment of my faith [or, the fulfillment of the Old Testament prophecies regarding the first appearance of Jesus on earth]). I think that they complement each other.

Christians and followers of Judaism both look forward to the coming of the Messiah. Christians believe that this will be a return appearance for the Messiah (Jesus). Followers of Judaism believe that this will be His first appearance.

For some, what follows is politically incorrect. No disrespect is intended. This regards Judaism not embracing the fulfillment of its faith (the New Testament). I have a story from the time of my pediatric residency that reminds me of the relationship between Judaism and Christianity (Judeo-Christianity). While the comparison is not accurate, you can probably see what I see in the story. It goes as follows: Dr. Bosley, who I believe was the first pediatrician in Grand Island, Nebraska, visited our residency program to give a presentation to the residents. The only thing that I remember from his presentation is a story about a family. The parents were very happy with the care that he provided for their child. And they were happy enough for one of them to say something along the lines of the following: "Dr. Bosley, we really like how you took care of our child. If only you had finished medical school, you could be our doctor, too!" They were apparently under the impression that the early parts of medical school dealt with learning about the medical problems of children, and that medical students didn't learn about the medical problems of adults until the later parts of medical school.

And here is some more political incorrectness: if you haven't embraced the fulfillment of your faith, or "finished medical school", so to speak, this is a humble invitation for you to consider doing so, and also a prayer that I ask you to consider.

> *"Dear God, I have been invited to examine my faith for the purpose of seeing if it needs remodeled and simplified. Please help me with this. Please help me to know if I should continue in my faith as it currently is, or should I embrace Jesus as my redeemer, the path to my salvation? Please help me to know if prophecies regarding the Messiah refer to Jesus of 2,000 years ago, or is He yet to make His first appearance? Please inspire me with the truth! Amen."*

Please think and pray about it, not for my benefit, but for yours. And, whether or not you are ever inspired to remodel your faith into Judeo-Christianity, I will always love you when I am under the influence of Jesus.

The case for church

Why join a church? Certainly, we can focus on our faith at home. We can read the Bible, pray, and discuss our faith with other family members while staying at home. And it is certainly easier to stay home than becoming active in a church. It is also less expensive.

What follows are some of the things that I find valuable about attending church.

First, I have come to the conclusion that my hour in church on Sunday is my best hour of the week. Of course, it helps that we have a truly inspirational pastor. He often says things that I have never thought of, things that help fill in the blanks of my faith knowledge. Or, he may say things that help reinforce conclusions that I have already reached. And it's not just knowledge that is valuable. The feeling that comes during his inspirational prayers can be truly powerful.

This truly powerful feeling of inspiration can also come from the hymns.

Being surrounded by people who share the same faith helps to reinforce and strengthen our faith. Paul, in 2 Timothy, chapter 2:22, says, "............: but follow righteousness, faith, charity, peace, with them that call on the Lord out of a pure heart."

Being a member of a church helps us more easily participate in the ministry of Jesus, both through financial offerings and service opportunities.

Church membership often offers additional and highly beneficial opportunities for education and fellowship. My Tuesday evening men's group, for example, has been way more helpful to me than I ever would have imagined it could be. Another benefit is that this type of activity leads to opportunities for friendships to develop.

For families with children, church membership offers many valuable faith-related opportunities for children.

Of course, if a family is diligent, most important church functions can be accomplished at home. But, with all of the demands of our modern lifestyle, it is often difficult to have the required level of diligence. The best, I think, would be a combination of church attendance and at-home activities to reinforce and strengthen our faith.

Catechism

It is vital that young Christians receive education regarding their faith. Catechism studies help fulfill this need. If a family belongs to a church, catechism classes can easily be attended. For families that don't belong to a church, catechism classes can be conducted at home. For this purpose, I would recommend Luther's Small Catechism, which is available online. This is the only catechism I am familiar with, but I find it hard to believe that a better one is available. Incidentally, Luther's introduction to his Small Catechism is interesting reading.

Looking back, I wish I would have reviewed our sons' catechism lessons with them at home. I think that reviewing this information together would have been good for all of us.

In (spiritual) fact(s), I have faith!

In Hebrews 11:1, Paul defines faith as "the substance of things hoped for, the evidence of things not seen." This is the definition that I learned in my catechism class growing up.

During one of my recent French lessons, I acquired a slightly different definition. The lesson covered the French word for facts. It was "faits". I immediately thought that it looks like faith. Based on that lesson and my personal experiences, faith now feels more like facts, to me. The experiences that I have told you about in 'Unusual occurrences' are definite facts to me, just as definite as anything in the rest of my life is. Two of these events were shared with other people ("5:42" was shared with my wife, and, of course, with Marvin; Miracle? was shared with the patient, the patient's mom, RN [the nurse], and one other nurse. For anyone else who didn't share in these experiences, the stories of these events probably aren't based on facts, as most people know facts to be. But to me, they are. They are based on "spiritual facts", my new, more clarified term for the type of facts to which I am referring. And my new motto could be, "In (spiritual) fact(s), I have faith!"

Another Inspirational French Lesson

Here is the story of another of my French lessons through Duolingo, an online system for language education. I clicked on the tab that says "practice weak skills", so I had no idea what the lesson would contain. I was trying to get through the lesson with reasonable speed because my wife and I were planning to leave for dinner at 5:30 PM (yes, we are AARP members). The lesson was pretty routine until I got to a sentence that I absolutely loved. The sentence, in English, was, "You have beautiful words!" I thought, "That's great!" I wondered if this could also have been directed to me beyond the lesson itself? I hoped so. You see, I had been having some doubts and concerns about my writing up until that point. I have prayed many times in the past few months a prayer that goes something like the following: "Lord, please help me write what is acceptable to You. Please give me inspiration. Please help me with the message and with the words! In Jesus' name, Amen."

The thought that perhaps this sentence was directed to me gave me a good feeling. 5:30 was approaching. I didn't want to make my lovely wife wait. The last sentence that I had to translate in the lesson was, in English, "It is necessary that we leave now." "Cool", I thought. I finished by 5:31, and then we left. We had a wonderful dinner, by the way, sitting outside and enjoying some of the finest weather in the world as we ate. I felt very fortunate, and I think my wife did, too.

An Image of Faith

I occasionally think of an image of faith for difficult times. My image is of a stormy sea, with passengers from a recently sunk ship swimming desperately to find something to cling to. One of the swimmers sees a somewhat tattered inflatable life raft appearing. Despite its first appearance not being too promising, he swims toward it anyway. As he gets closer, it appears more sound than he first thought; he believes that this raft might offer the hope he is looking for. Then he notes the name on the side; it isn't clear because it is faded, and a couple of letters are missing, but it looks something like "B l ef". He briefly wonders what the full word was. He struggles to climb on board. A couple other passengers are already there. They appear weak and exhausted, but also relieved. Then our swimmer finds a place to sit and rest.

He looks around, familiarizing himself with his rescue raft. He then notices a little tag sown into the seam of the raft. He moves a little closer to see what the label says. He then sees "Hope Floatation Products, Inc." on the label. Interesting, he thinks to himself, as he now realizes that he, too, has hope. He reclines against the side of the raft. He starts to look around. He sees another swimmer in the water nearby. He sits upright and yells, "Swim over here! We have room for you!" The nearby swimmer answers back, with some difficulty, "I don't.... like the looks of .....your raft...... it looks... like....it will sink....I think I... can...do better!" So he swims on past. Our recently rescued swimmer tries to urge him to come back, again and again, but soon the other swimmer is out of range for hearing. "Too bad", he says. The others agree.

He then notices something that he hadn't noticed before. A thin cable is attached to the raft. He moves closer to inspect the cable. The cable is taught. He isn't sure where it leads to because visibility isn't good in the agitated sea. Then he notices a little label attached to the line. He can see that it says, "Faith Fibers, Inc." "Hmmmm", he says to himself. He then realizes that he is exhausted, so he lies down to rest......The next thing he knows is another person lying next to him, also wet and exhausted. He then looks up and sees a strong man ready to climb off the raft and back into the water. Our rescued swimmer says, "Don't go!" The strong rescuer turns around and calmly but confidently says, "Fear not! I will return for you and your fellow passengers. You will be brought back to our ship. It is unsinkable! Now I need to go. I must search for more people who need rescuing." Our man replies, "OK, it looks like you are more than up to the task...Oh....and thanks!"

The rescuer strongly swims away, and is soon out of sight. Our man and the others resume their rest. Then, when he feels a little stronger, he sits up and looks out into the still stormy sea. Soon, his jaw drops simultaneously with a gasp, and then he starts rubbing his eyes. "What's wrong?" asks one of the fellow passengers. Our man replies, "My eyes must have been playing tricks on me. For a moment, I thought I saw someone walking on water"...

Crumbs from the table

You're probably familiar with this story from the New Testament. It is one of my favorites because of the inspirational nature of the great faith of the woman in the story. You can read the story in Matthew 15:22–28, but I will briefly tell it. A woman from Canaan sought help from Jesus for her daughter, who was "grievously vexed with a devil." Jesus initially ignored her pleas for help, but when she persisted, He told her that "I am not sent but unto the lost sheep of the house of Israel." She didn't give up. He then replied, "It is not meet to take the children's bread and cast it to the dogs." She replied, "Truth, Lord: yet the dogs eat of the crumbs which fall from their master's table." Jesus then answered her this way, "O woman, great is thy faith: be it unto thee as thou wilt." And her daughter was cured ("made whole") at that point.

Of course, Jesus knew that He was sent to earth for everyone, not just for the people of Israel. But the way that He interacted with her and spoke with her provided a good test of her faith.

I like to think of this woman's story in regard to heaven. I don't know if there is any type of hierarchy for us in heaven, but if there is, I will be OK with it. Even the "crumbs from the table" level in heaven will be much better than what we experience in our present world, and certainly vastly better than what is in store for us if we don't get to heaven. So now my goal is to attain the "crumbs from the table" level in heaven, while of course being willing to accept anything better that God may have in store for me.

A faith of convenience?

Our pastor once addressed this issue. Do we have a faith of convenience, or are we fully engaged in our faith? Too often we plan our faith activities just as we plan our other activities for the week. We want to keep our faith participation limited to the one, two, or however many hours we have allotted for it. To devote more hours to it would be inconvenient. If we have all of these other demands on our time, how can we possibly devote more time to our faith? I admit that my faith has often been a faith of convenience.

I can now tell you that this (writing that I am doing) is the closest that I have ever been to having an inconvenient faith. You might think, "What's the problem? You have all sorts of time on your hands." True enough. But I am stepping out of my box of safety, so to speak. I am not used to communicating about my faith. And I am missing some of March Madness. But let me tell you, the closer I get to having an inconvenient faith, the better I feel! I have never before felt such inspiration for any task! And I never before have felt such sustained peace! (Now, what would truly be a faith of inconvenience for me would be having to communicate all of my faith-related thoughts by speaking before an audience!)

We must remember that we have much more time for our faith than we think that we do. We find this extra time for our faith by living our faith. If we let ourselves be inspired to live according to the example of Jesus, the problem will be solved! And our new-found inconvenient faith won't feel inconvenient at all!

Promotion by demotion

This involves the concept of putting God first in our lives. God's Word in the Bible tells us numerous times that we should do this. God should be ranked ahead of anyone we can think of (ourselves, our spouses, our children, our parents, our siblings, our friends, etc., etc.). And we ourselves should not be ranked above our family, friends, or anyone else. This, at first, might seem a little demanding of God. But He knows what He is doing in making this demand of us. And I don't think He makes this demand because He craves more attention, as we might. I think He makes this demand simply for our benefit. He knows how we work. He designed us, for Heaven's sake! (I think this is an acceptable use of an expression that is often used as an oath, by the way). He knows that if we truly honor Him, we will follow His wishes on how we should live (i.e., we will follow the example that Jesus gave us).

God's perfection is so much above our sorry state that by simply ranking him Number 1, He pulls us closer to His level (remember the Bible verse I mentioned earlier, James 4:8. It reads, "Draw nigh to God and He will draw nigh to you). In other words, we, our families, and our friends are promoted to a higher level than the one in which we would otherwise be. This, in turn, will lead to happier, less stressful, and less depressing lives for all of us. Oh, Yahoo!

Another way of titling this chapter might be "Who's in charge?" or "A child-like faith". These thoughts came to me a day or two after I recently started praying for a child-like faith, in addition to the simple and strong faith that I had been requesting for several years. It occurred to me that children feel reassurance from having someone strong and powerful (their parents) watching over them, and being in charge of their lives. They feel secure and loved. And they trust and love their parents in return, and want to be helpful to their parents. And even when they misbehave, they feel some security in knowing what their limits for misbehavior are. If we rank God number one in our lives, we have this feeling of love and security, and we trust and love Him in return. If we don't put Him in first place, we miss out on these benefits, the benefits of a child-like faith!

(I'm writing this on Palm Sunday, 2016, a few days after I wrote what you just read. It just occurred to me that parents enjoy playing with their children, and vice versa. This also can be part of our child-like faith. While in church today, my imagination took me to the same place that it has periodically visited since we started going to our church. We have a beautiful stained glass window located high in a recessed space above the part that might be called the chancel, the area where the pastor, musicians, and singers are located during the service [Our church doesn't have a traditional design; the area that I describe could also simply be called the stage]. Below the stained-glass window is a long, sloped area, with a slope similar to that of a steep slide. The sloped area widens with descent. The lowest part of the slope is the closest part to the stage and the congregation. This sloped area is covered with drywall and is painted white. The bottom of the slope is just a short distance behind and above the musicians and singers. When our pastor invites God to fill our sanctuary with His presence [or words similar to that], I like to imagine God entering through the stained-glass window and sliding down the slope so that He can join His people in the sanctuary. Of course, He can enter however He wants to, but then, I tell myself, maybe He enters the way that I imagine simply to make me happy! In my mind, this is an image of happiness and playfulness, and it works for me! So, maybe I have had a child-like faith longer than I have realized. I sense that there is a lot of joy available to us if we allow our faith to be transformed into the faith of a child).

Predestination vs. free will, and the Elect

Many people believe that all of the world's events are predestined or predetermined by God the Father. I do not believe that God works this way most of the time, but there are some exceptions, such as Jesus' first appearance on earth and His plans for Jesus' second appearance on earth. Of course, none of us truly knows the full extent of God's participation in earthly events. That said, I do feel that God the Father knows everything that will happen and when it will happen. Some interpret this ability of God (to know future events) as proof of predestination. I think that God, through the Holy Spirit, gives us plenty of nudges in a positive direction, but I do not believe that He is a "puppet-master" who micromanages our existence.

I think that the balance between good and evil is inherent in creating something from nothing (see Physics of Faith for further thoughts on this). And I think that it is because of this balance that we were given free will and the ability to be influenced by the forces of good and forces of evil. With free will we have a choice, and it appears that none of us is capable of resisting the influences of evil to any great degree. This results in all of us becoming polluted by evil. As a result, all of us need the cleansing forgiveness and the redemption that is provided by God's plan of salvation (Jesus' victory over death and damnation for us). Fortunately for us, our free will enables us to accept and embrace God's plan of salvation, and thereby overcome the downside of the balance between good and evil. It therefore makes more sense to me that our existence operates according to free will than to predestination.

The use of the designation "the elect" in the Bible,

referring to those who will be saved, probably also makes a lot of people believe in predestination. I believe that "the elect" is used by God to refer to those whom He already knows will join Him in heaven, but I don't think that it has anything to do with Him deciding who will be there with Him, for the most part (there may be some exceptions). I think that He has always known who will be with Him in heaven because of His perfect knowledge of the future. I think that God would like us all to be "the elect", but He knew from the beginning that some wouldn't be joining Him (unfortunately, because of free will, they would reject His plan of salvation).

If there is a balance between good and evil, does that mean that half of the population won't receive salvation? No, not necessarily. Even the greatest devotee to evil has the free will to reject evil and grasp onto a redeeming faith in Jesus. One can be a very evil person by human standards, but if he or she becomes a follower of Jesus for the remainder of his or her life and is penitent, he or she will receive salvation. And only God knows who will receive salvation and who will not.

So, after all that, is this necessary to know? Most of the information in the previous paragraph, specifically the last three sentences, is necessary to know, but the rest is mostly unnecessary. I feel certain of that. And the earlier statements in this part may not be entirely correct, anyway (I feel that they are, but this is only my opinion). Then why did I write it? Mainly to try to dismiss the idea of predestination. I think that the idea of predestination is incorrect, and it also is a little demoralizing, as it makes some people think, "Why bother with faith if everything is predetermined?"

So there! Renew your faith and keep it! Salvation is available to all; that's the first part of the equation resulting in eternal life with God. The second part? Find your faith in Jesus, God the Father, and the Holy Spirit, then securely grasp onto this faith and never let go! (In another part, Things Best Left to God, I will address those who haven't heard about Jesus).

Things of this world

I don't remember how old I was when I became aware of this concept from the Bible (probably about 12 or 13), but I do remember that right away it appealed to me. Since then I have periodically thought of this and I have tried not to get overly concerned about or attached to "worldly" things. The Bible verses that address this concept are Colossians 3:2 and 1 John 2:15–17. Colossians says, "Set your affection on things above, not on things of the earth." The words in 1 John are, "Love not the world, neither the things that are in the world. If any man love the world, the love of the Father is not in him. For all that is in the world, the lust of the flesh, and the lust of the eyes, and the pride of life, is not of the Father, but is of the world. And the world passeth away, and the lust thereof: but he that doeth the will of God abideth forever."

You can see that there is some overlap between this idea and that of the Bible verses that I quote in Long Term Investing. And I don't think that the words, "Love not the world" are against an environmentally conscious attitude (in case you couldn't already tell, I am a "greenie" and a "tree-hugger"). This idea concerns our addictions or "idols" that get in the way of us connecting with God and living as Jesus taught us to live (....although one can probably even take "being a greenie" too far, and this, too, could become one's "idol" or addiction).

I don't think that we should detach completely from the things of this world. We should be sufficiently connected to the world to be able to interact with the rest of mankind in the manner that God wants us to (i.e., to follow the idea of living according to the question "What would Jesus do?" and actually doing what His words and examples have taught us). We wouldn't do much good by fully shunning society and living as hermits; doing so would definitely not allow us to live as Jesus would have us live!

Not getting too caught up in the things of this world not only helps get us to the right place for the remainder of our existence, it also helps us in this life. This can be part of our stress management plan. It can be highly stressful to try to keep up with modern pop culture, all of our modern toys, gadgets, and games, and modern temptations, not to mention all of the old temptations that are still around. My current "poster child" image for our modern culture is the sad image of a teenager or adult being led about by a "modern device", held in hand while walking, with neck flexed and eyes unwaveringly and adoringly fixed on the device, and seemingly oblivious to the rest of the world. Although they are unlikely to admit feeling stressed, I suspect that people in this position subconsciously fear missing out on great information. I also suspect that they find admiring and communing with nature too old-fashioned – something they have little time for.

Anyway, you probably get my point. I think that when we too fully embrace the things of this world, we miss out on a lot of goodness and peace that is otherwise available to us.

Things best left to God

A few things are best left for God to decide – things that we aren't qualified to decide, or even speak about. These include judgements about another person's faith, or lack of faith, or about a person's ultimate destination in the hereafter.

Regarding another person's faith, God is the ultimate judge since we cannot see into another's heart, mind, or soul. We should not spread rumors about a person's faith being something other than what that person claims it is. Don't we think that our God is capable of deciding for Himself what a person believes?

Regarding a person's destination in the hereafter, we are also incapable of knowing or deciding about that. Keeping our own lives and faith in order is challenging enough, so we have no business trying to decide the outcome for someone else. God is more than capable of this task on His own without our meager help!

One concern that we sometimes hear centers on what happens to those who never received the good news of salvation that is available to us through faith in Jesus. This hasn't been revealed to me, and I doubt if anyone is truly qualified to answer this. This is also an issue for God to resolve, and not for us. What is our concern, however, is that we are called to spread the good news about Jesus whenever and wherever possible.

Our Interactions with People of Other Faiths

Those of us who are Christians (or Judeo-Christians, as I like to think of us) should not shy away from people of other faiths, or from those who have no faith. We should treat them as Jesus would, with respect and love, and we should be sure that we are living our faith gently but confidently in their presence. We should live as "lights of the world", including and especially when we are in their presence. Remember that we would likely have their faith, or lack of faith, if we had the same upbringing and life experiences that they have had. This should help us to understand and respect why their faith may differ from ours, or why they may have no faith at all. We should remain open to talking about our faith in a gentle and loving but also confident manner when the opportunity arises. They may have doubts about their faith, or lack of faith, and want to find out about ours. I am certain that God does not want us to miss these opportunities.

We can find words in the Bible that support the preceding thoughts. Second Timothy, 2:24–26 says, "And the servant of the Lord must not strive; but be gentle unto all men, apt to teach, patient, In meekness instructing those that oppose themselves; if God peradventure will give them repentance to the acknowledging of the truth; And that they may recover themselves out of the snare of the devil, who are taken captive by him at his will."

To those whose faith is not the same as mine, I respect that your faith is different from mine. Your faith would likely be my faith if I had had the same upbringing and life experiences that you have had. And I not only respect you, but I sometimes love you (when I am under the influence of Jesus, I love you, but when I am under the influence of Satan, I don't love you). I invite you to find out more about my faith. Here is a prayer for you to consider praying: "Dear God, I have been invited to learn more about the writer's faith, the faith in Jesus Christ, God the Father, and the Holy Spirit (the Holy Trinity). Have I already been inspired to come this far? Please help me with this. Please give me inspiration about the true faith, the way that You want me to connect with You. As I read and consider the words of Jesus in the New Testament with an open mind, please inspire me to know the direction I should take. Is the faith of the New Testament the true faith? I need Your help with this. Please help me, Lord! Amen."

To those who have no faith, I respect that you have no faith. Your lack of faith would likely be my lack of faith if I shared your upbringing and life experiences. Not only do I respect you, I sometimes love you (when I am under the influence of Jesus, I love you, but when I am under the influence of Satan, I don't love you). I invite you, also, to find out more about my faith. You may have been inspired to read this far. Here is a prayer for you to consider praying: "Dear God, I'm not sure that You even exist, but if You do, please inspire me. Please be with me as I, with an open mind, read and consider the words of Jesus in the New Testament. Please inspire me regarding Your existence, and also regarding whether or not I should embrace Jesus as my Redeemer. I need help with this. Please help me, Lord! Amen."

Is Salvation Available to Those Who Don't Believe in Jesus?

If we believe in Jesus, we believe what He tells us in the New Testament. And He addresses salvation in John 3:17 and 18, which says, "For God sent not His Son into the world to condemn the world; but that the world through Him might be saved. He that believeth on Him is not condemned: but he that believeth not is condemned already, because he hath not believed in the name of the only begotten Son of God." This tells me that salvation isn't available to those who don't believe in Jesus. The important message to me is that we are all condemned unless we accept Jesus as our Redeemer. Rejecting Jesus doesn't result in extra punishment; if we reject Jesus, we simply continue on the same path that we were already taking, the path to damnation. It is basically a "take it or leave it" situation; it is up to us to accept Him, or not accept Him. I suspect that God (our Holy Trinity) is much more sad than angry when Jesus is rejected, like a firefighter whose rescue efforts are refused by someone who is heading to certain doom.

Another thought regarding the availability of salvation to people of other faiths is this. If salvation is available through means other than our faith in Jesus, it wasn't necessary for Jesus be sent to earth to earn our salvation. Our faith is a hoax if salvation is available by other means! (And I know that it is not a hoax!) Instead of sending His own Son to earn our salvation, God the Father could simply have revealed that one could go 500 miles east to find out about Joe's religion, since his religion appeared acceptable to God. Or, one could travel 700 miles SSW to find out about Ed's religion, which was another acceptable path to salvation. If we believe that there are other paths to salvation besides Christianity, then we do not believe the words of Jesus! Here I am simply stating the message of the New Testament. Of course, I would like everyone to be saved, even through their non-Christian faith. But this is not what Jesus revealed to us!

That being said, the wisdom of God is beyond our human understanding. He doesn't need our help in deciding who is saved and who isn't. But, if there is another path to salvation, it hasn't been revealed to me. So, I think that the wisest course of action for anyone who has been told about Jesus is to find out more about Him by reading, with an open mind, His words in the New Testament, and to pray frequently for inspiration one way or the other regarding this question, "Is this the true faith?"

Why do we do good works?

Doing good works seems to be a vital part of our Christian faith (or Judeo-Christian faith, as I like to think of it). But since our path to salvation doesn't involve good works, why do we do them?

This is also a question that I have pondered intermittently for years. And like the question, "Why do we worship God?", it became easier for me to be blessed with answers when I focused on the loving nature of God. I think there are at least three reasons why we do good works, and they overlap to some degree. One of them has to do with a command from Jesus. The other two have more to do with us. The reason that has to do with Jesus' command is that we are called to be lights unto the world in order to help more people see that they should glorify God (and, in turn, become followers of Jesus). Matthew 5: 14–16 says, "Ye are the light of the world. A city that is set on a hill cannot be hid. Neither do men light a candle and put it under a bushel, but on a candlestick; and it giveth light unto all that are in the house. Let your light so shine before men, that they may see your good works, and glorify your Father, which is in heaven."

The reasons that have to do with us involve celebration and monitoring our faith. Good works and celebration? How does that work? When we have something really great happen to or for us, we naturally like to celebrate. It is fun to celebrate. It seems to prolong the good feelings that we have. Often we choose to dine at a great restaurant as a means of celebration. Sometimes we choose less safe means of celebrating, such as, "getting wasted" by overconsuming alcohol. Regardless of the means, we want the good feelings to continue.

So how does doing good works come into play? Well, I'm sure that you recall being helpful to someone, and feeling really good about it, even though he or she was the beneficiary of your good works. And the good feelings from this type of celebration are usually stronger and last longer than those derived from other types of celebration. The good feelings that we derive from doing good works keep the original good feelings going. And what were these good feelings from, in the first place? Why are we celebrating at all? Because of the great news that we have received in God's plan of salvation! So, one way of looking at this is that the best way for us to celebrate our good news about Jesus is doing good for others, which helps prolong our good feelings. And, you know what, our means of celebration also helps us follow Jesus' command to "let our light shine before men". This, in turn, helps prolong our good feelings, so we feel like celebrating more by doing more good works…and so on, and so on. It gets a little dizzying to think that we can have a never-ending supply of good feelings if we step into these series of cycles! What a shining light we would be! Oh, Yahoo!

And what about the other reason, monitoring our faith? How does that work? It works this way: if we don't feel like celebrating the good news about Jesus by doing good works, we have to be suspicious that perhaps the strength of our faith isn't where it should be. What does one do if that's the case? We have to examine our lives to see if something is getting in the way of our faith development (is there some type of idol or addiction getting in the way, for example?). And we have to nourish and strengthen our faith by some, or preferably all, of the following: prayer, reading God's word, fellowship with other Christians, and even fellowship with non-Christians, by "living our faith" in their presence and being ready, of course, to gently but confidently witness for our faith if there is an opening to do so. Incidentally, these are all things that we should be proactively doing anyway, for purposes of faith preservation.

"Enough, already!!!"

This part concerns the "end times." This is often a scary topic for Christians. I admit that it has been for me as well, but I am glad to say that it has gradually become less and less scary for me. The Bible frequently tells us, "Fear not." Here I write of my personal journey to a state of not fearing the "end times."

One day God the Father will decide, "Enough, already!!!" That will be the time that the world will meet Jesus again! And that is when Jesus will start what I like to think of as the great separation of good and evil.

From my late childhood until halfway through my teenage years, my family would frequently listen to a radio program called "The World Tomorrow." The speaker was Garner Ted Armstrong. He spoke about Biblical prophecies pertaining to the "end times." I think that we all found it interesting. Sometimes I found it to be a little scary, but usually not too scary. Armstrong was not a passionate speaker, but he was an interesting speaker. To me, he sounded like an eloquent college professor who really knew his stuff. He quite easily kept our attention.

I found the messages on prophecies interesting, but I didn't dwell on them. That is, not until June of 1967, when I was 14. That is when the Six Day War occurred. This was an Arab-Israeli conflict. With the news of this conflict, I felt more than a little stunned. I already knew that I didn't like war, but it was more than that. It seemed to me that the "end times" prophecies were being manifested in our time. For days, I felt gloomy about the prophecies and seemingly associated events. At that point and for years afterward, thinking of the "end times" provoked a little fear in me, so I usually tried to keep my thoughts from going there.

Ever since the Six Day War, whenever the Middle East experiences war or other troublesome events, I feel that my "radar" for that region starts sending stronger signals to my consciousness and sub-consciousness. My mood used to become more somber, which carried a mild visceral component, and I would remain alert to news from the region. As an adult, I have often wondered if being equipped with this "radar" is just a byproduct of me having listened to programs on Biblical prophecy when I was younger, or if there truly is something connected to it. Or perhaps it's both.

Ever since Jesus' first appearance on earth, at least some of his followers have believed that they were living in the "end times." From our perspective, they were wrong, unless one wants to consider all time between Jesus' first appearance and his second coming to be the "end times."

From my adolescence until late forties, I generally thought that God would cause the "end times" events that are described in the Bible. During those years, I also did not read the Bible all that much. In the past ten to fifteen years, I have been gradually (slowly but surely) blessed with an outlook that causes me to avoid dwelling as much on these events as I did earlier, at least in a negative sense. My "radar" for the Middle East is still very functional, and I still follow the news from the region somewhat closely, but I no longer feel the negative effects. I feel that my ability to focus beyond worldly events and more on God and His plans for us is a gift from God. Thinking of this ability as a gift has helped me to contemplate the "end times" with much less fear. I think that this blessing is God's response to my increased prayer, especially my prayer for a simple, strong, and child-like faith, along with my increased contemplation about Him.

Today, I believe that God has not and will not cause all of the "end times" events that we read about in the Bible. I believe that some of the events will be caused by God, but that many have been and will continue to be caused by mankind, including events related to climate change, warfare and other human-caused atrocities and disasters. I also believe that Satan will continue to play a major role in many of the "end times" events. I believe that God is not trying to scare us with the "end times" prophecies, but is simply giving us a "heads up", so to speak, because He loves us and doesn't want our faith to weaken during the increasingly difficult times that were prophesied. I believe that God knows exactly what will happen and exactly when it will happen, but that doesn't mean He will cause of all of these events.

No one, other than God the Father, knows when all of the prophesied events will take place. There is good reason for this. God wants us to continue living full lives according to His Will. It's not difficult to imagine how we would alter our behavior and our thoughts if we knew exactly when these events would occur. This is probably why the prophecies are difficult for me and many others to understand; if we completely understood the prophecies, including the exact timing of events, we might deviate from the lives that God wants us to live and from the strong faith and watchfulness that He wants us to maintain. With this kind of knowledge, we would likely be tempted to relax in our efforts to maintain our strong faith until it seemed more necessary for us to have a strong faith. We might think that we could have fun now [with sin] and still have plenty of time to get our faith in order later. This type of thinking would put us at risk for losing our faith!

We should have no doubt about the "end times" prophecies. After all, the Old Testament prophecies of Jesus' first appearance on earth were absolutely fulfilled.

An important prophecy to watch for is the rebuilding of the temple in Jerusalem. This should be a signal to us to renew our efforts to become more aware of other prophecies and to watch for their fulfillment. Of course, we should not wait for this event. Now is the time to get our faith completely in order!

A few years ago, during a phone conversation Marvin told me, "Uncle Wilbur thinks that we are living in the 'end days.'" I then replied, "I have felt that way for a long time." My response was mostly due to my many Middle East "radar" activations over a number of years, which I previously mentioned. But it was also partly motivated by my growing belief that humans, while under varying degrees of influence from Satan, are the cause of the vast majority of negative "end times" events.

The first part of Second Timothy, chapter three, describes the behavioral characteristics of many people during the "end times." If you read this, you can see that this describes much of our present world. In the same chapter, verses 14–16 tell us of the antidote against the poisonous behaviors and influences of the "end times." And Second Peter, chapter three, addresses the "scoffers" in the "end times," those who doubt the return of Jesus. This chapter also addresses the attitude and watchfulness that Jesus wants us to have regarding His return.

Given the ever-increasing number of events caused by humans that portend the "end times", I think that we are living in a time when it is realistic to ask, "Will I meet Jesus while I am still alive, or when I die?" Since the age of fourteen I have often felt that my meeting with Him is likely to occur while I am alive.

I used to think that if we simply stayed strong in the faith, we wouldn't have to be very aware of the "end times" prophecies. But now I think that God wants us to have a good awareness of the prophecies so that our faith isn't overwhelmed by fear during these difficult times and events, so that we aren't misled by Satan or anyone else claiming to be Jesus, and so that our faith can be strengthened as we watch and see the prophesied events unfolding. Regarding Jesus' return, we will know that Jesus has not returned until we see Him "coming in the clouds of heaven with power and great glory" [Matthew 24:30]. The entire world will be aware of Jesus' return at once; of this there will be no doubt! If our focus is solely on the present world, we will likely have plenty to fear. But if we instead focus on what is greater, namely, God and His plans for us, we will have far less to fear. God wants us to stay alert and stay strong in the faith until He gathers us for our trip Home with Him! We must always keep this belief in heart, mind, and soul!!!

The Holy Trinity

Many people, including those who have the Christian faith, those with another faith, and those without any faith, are confused about the Holy Trinity. Why is God divided into three "persons?"

I have several thoughts on this. First, God truly is one God (John 17:22 gives us an example of Jesus telling us this, "And the glory which thou gavest me I have given them; that they may be one, just as We are one;"). God chose to divide into three persons not for His sake, but for our sake. The ways in which He interacts with us are more understandable to us with this division of labor:

- God the Father responsible for creation, law giving, administration, etc.
- Jesus, God the Son for teaching, salvation, shepherding, etc.
- God the Holy Spirit for inspiration, comforting, and guidance, as well as for connecting us with the Father and Son.

God could have just as easily performed all of these functions without subdividing into three persons, but it is a lot easier for us to understand His interactions with us in this subdivided manner. And by subdividing for us, He is practicing what He preaches!

Second, God's personal division of labor is instructive for us, His children, for application to our own daily lives. Sometimes we must be self-reliant, but, whenever and wherever possible and appropriate, we should work cooperatively with others according to His example. This allows people to work in the areas in which they excel, and, as a result, all of us benefit.

I used to try to understand God the Father, God the Son (Jesus), and God the Holy Spirit strictly in terms of what

I read in the Bible. But, for me, there were blanks in the images provided by this method. More and more, in recent years, my imagination has helped to fill in some of those blanks by drawing from human sources. Before you start thinking that this sounds disrespectful or even heretical, remember that we are told that we have been created in God's image. And I have tried to remove the parts of my human images that operate under the influence of Satan.

This method allows me to think of God the Father as a perfect and holy renaissance man. He is the ultimate scientist, engineer, architect, biologist, chemist, physicist, environmental scientist, farmer, rancher, zookeeper, park ranger, conservationist, physician, nurse, psychologist, philosopher, teacher, historian, military general, statesman, writer, librarian, computer geek, clockmaker, aesthetician, lawgiver, administrator, judge, lawyer, ethicist, social worker, artist, sculptor, educator, laborer, factory worker, construction worker, secretary, plumber, maid, homemaker, and parent, all in one form. You may have noticed that my list doesn't include politician, because politics isn't needed for God's role of lawgiving. God the Father and Jesus might more appropriately be considered negotiators than politicians (regarding our prayer requests to them, the creation of Old Testament covenants, and Jesus speaking to His Father on our behalf). I am certain that I left out many roles that should be on the list.

The human image that I think of when I think of God the Father is Ben Franklin. And I think especially of the Ben Franklin who said, "Beer is proof that God loves us and wants us to be happy." You see, I think that God (the entire Holy Trinity) truly does love us and truly does want us to be happy. Of course, God the Father doesn't have Ben Franklin's human weaknesses. He doesn't operate under the influence of Satan. (Regarding beer, God is probably OK with us drinking beer in moderation for the purpose suggested by Ben Franklin [Think of Jesus making wine from water for the wedding at Cana, in Galilee.], but I am rather certain that He doesn't want us to go beyond moderation [Satan is the one who derives pleasure from us drinking beyond moderation.]).

To further clarify, Ben Franklin is my image of God the Father when He is happy. But He isn't always happy, as we have read many times in the Bible (mostly the Old Testament, it seems). To help me imagine God the Father when He is angry, I think of His face morphing from Ben Franklin's image to that of a stern George Washington.

The Holy Spirit has always been a little more difficult for me to understand. In several different Bible verses He has been referred to as the Comforter. He seems to be our connection to God the Father and God the Son (Jesus). John 15:26 says, "But when the Comforter is come, whom I will send unto you from the Father, even the Spirit of truth, which proceedeth from the Father, he shall testify of me." To me, this fits with the following words about the Holy Spirit in the Nicene Creed, "who proceeds from the Father and the Son." He proceeds from both the Father and the Son because Jesus has a role in sending the Holy Spirit to us, as you can see in the verse above. The Nicene Creed goes on to say that the Holy Spirit "together with the Father and the Son is worshipped and glorified."

Since I started thinking of the Holy Spirit as our connection to the Father and the Son, I have used computers and the internet as models to help understand Him. Initially, I liked to think of Him as the original, and still the best, internet. Now I often think of Him as an app that we are equipped with and that should ideally be engaged at all times. Sometimes I like to think of Him as the ultimate computer nerd (no disrespect intended) who can connect all believers to the Father and the Son, and vice versa.

Regarding the advice or influence that we get or feel from the Holy Spirit, I like to think of these words from the Kenny Rogers song, "The Gambler":

> *You've got to know when to hold 'em, know when to fold 'em, know when to walk away, and know when to run. You never count your money when your sittin' at the table. There'll be time enough for countin' when the dealin's done.*
>
> *Every gambler knows that the secret to survivin' is knowin' what to throw away and knowin' what to keep. 'Cause every hand's a winner and every hand's a loser, and the best that you can hope for is to die in your sleep.*

(This is much more effective, incidentally, if you listen to it as sung by Kenny Rogers, himself!)

For a long time, I have felt that this song is loaded with spiritual meaning, and I don't think it takes too much of a "leap of faith" to apply a lot of it to our faith. Of course, the Holy Spirit isn't interested in helping us with gambling, except for wanting to keep us from immersing ourselves in it.

The previous example might suggest that the Holy Spirit's main job is to keep us out of trouble. That is just one of His duties. I believe that He also gives us lots of positive nudges toward good, or "What would Jesus do?" actions. Some of those positive nudges come in bigger and more obvious forms, such as those that got me started on this project.

This final thought on the Holy Spirit came to me as I thought more about two Bible verses that I have cited elsewhere in this book. One is John 16:13, "Howbeit when he, the Spirit of truth, is come, he will guide you into all truth: for he shall not speak of himself; but whatsoever he shall hear, that shall he speak: and he will show you things to come." The other is John 6:12, which teaches us that Jesus doesn't want us to waste: "Gather up the fragments that remain, that nothing be lost." The first verse indicates to me that the Holy Spirit might utilize stored information that was made available beforehand ("but whatsoever he shall hear"). Jesus' disciples wouldn't have been aware of the concept of information storage within us, beyond our memories. The phrase, "but whatsoever he shall hear" would have sufficed as a substitute for pre-stored information available to the Holy Spirit.

In this way, I can more easily think of my personal share of the Holy Spirit as an app that can access information about my life. I like to think that this information, available to the Holy Spirit, as needed, may have been stored in me well before it was needed (likely at conception). And where could it be stored? How about in our DNA? There are great sections of DNA for which scientists haven't been able to assign functions. That's where the second verse applies. Since He teaches us not to waste, God wouldn't have created vast stretches of DNA with no purpose. So, I suggest that these parts of DNA without known functions might be storage areas for life information available to our Holy Spirit apps! Of course, with God's limitless capabilities, His information storage methods wouldn't be limited to just the seemingly unused parts of our DNA. And, of course, it may be unnecessary for such life information to be stored within us; Jesus and/or God the Father can communicate directly with the Holy Spirit, as needed, thereby bypassing the need for stored information.

Like the Physics of Faith questions, this is just another thing that is fun to think about – something that is unlikely to be refuted and impossible for me to prove.

Regarding Jesus, we don't have as many blanks to fill because He is so well documented in the New Testament. But, of course, we don't know what he looked like. Obviously, several painters have depicted Him, and we can accept those images of Him if we choose. Another possible way for us to envision Him is to imagine Him with the face of anyone in our family or group of friends, but only when that person is living according to the question, "What would Jesus do?" Our image should be of that person being happy, and laughing and smiling, as often as is appropriate for the circumstances, while being helpful and providing loving reassurance and wisdom to others. This image of Jesus works for me!

Or, maybe we do know what He looked like! If you are interested, you can watch Myth Hunters, Season 3, Episode 2, which is titled The Veil of Veronica. (Here Veronica doesn't refer to a person; it is simply the Latin word for true icon). In this fascinating program, we possibly see the image of Jesus' face on an ancient cloth that may have been the facial part of His burial shrouds. If it is true, then it was likely a photograph of Jesus that was supernaturally produced at the instant of His resurrection. And if you are starting to think, "Is this even possible?", remember that for God, everything is possible and nothing is impossible!

As a child, I was moderately fearful of God the Father, Jesus, and the Holy Spirit. Now, I am not so fearful of God, but I have a healthy respect for Him and love of Him, and I know that we should have proper humility when praying to Him or thinking about Him. The only fear that we should have regarding God is the fear of losing our faith in God, and its consequences for us.

A few words about Satan

People nowadays don't speak much about Satan. Of course, we don't speak much about God, either. Many people don't believe that Satan exists. They like to think of evil things as being due to human nature, and not due to us being tempted by Satan.

I do believe that Satan exists. On many occasions, Jesus spoke of Satan. Three of the gospels tell us of Jesus fasting for forty days in the Judaean Desert after He was baptized. During this time, Satan tempted Him many times. If we believe the words of Jesus, we believe that Satan exists (while the Old Testament also mentions Satan, the New Testament does so much more frequently).

If Satan exists, wouldn't he be more obvious to us? Imagine for a moment that he was obvious. In that case, don't you think that his presence would literally scare the hell out of most of us? We would quickly be running to Jesus if he made us more aware of himself!

Satan seems to be very "good" at his job of being very bad. He makes sin fun for us, at least in the early stages of it. He makes it easy for us to confuse what is sinful and what is holy. He makes our minds wander, and fills us with doubt. And he is relentless in all of this. That is why we need to fill our hearts, minds, and souls with the thoughts of Jesus, or, the entire Holy Trinity, as much as possible. Doing so will give Satan will fewer opportunities to lead us astray.

See 'Physics of faith' for my thoughts on Satan as they relate to the apparent balance of good and evil in the world.

My thoughts on the Lord's Prayer

Luther's Small Catechism, available online, contains some excellent thoughts on the Lord's Prayer, but I have a few additions to what he says. I think that "Hallowed be Thy Name" means that we should have utmost respect for the Name of God. This is the same concept that is stated in the second[1] of the Ten Commandments: Thou shalt not take the Name of the Lord thy God in vain. We should not use "God" casually or in "un-hallowed" ways in our speech. We are all guilty of not living up to this; our pervasive use of "God damn it!", "Jeeesuuuuus Christ!" and "Oh.........my.........God!", in all their variations, are prime examples. We should reserve our use of "God", "Jesus", "Jesus Christ", and "Holy Spirit" or "Holy Ghost" in our speech or thoughts for prayer, praise, or for respectful thoughts or discussions about God. If we don't respect the Name of God, will we respect God (Father, Son, and Holy Spirit) enough to have adequate faith during our prayers? Or will our praise of God mean anything to us? And if it doesn't mean anything to us, will it mean anything to God? I suspect that God is as upset and saddened, and probably more upset and saddened by this effect of using His Name in an unhallowed manner than He is by any insult to Him. Rather than using it carelessly, a good start for us would be to use God's Name respectfully – in prayer, praise, serious thoughts about God, or serious discussions about God with other people.

When we pray, "Thy Kingdom come", I think that we are actually praying for the end of our current earthly

---

[1] Martin Luther maintained the numbering of the commandments established by St. Augustine; other Protestant churches along with Eastern Orthodoxy use a numbering that aligns with the Jewish tradition in which this is the third of the Ten Commandments.

existence. Another way of saying this is that we are praying for the Second Coming of Jesus. When I first realized this, it was a very sobering thought for me. But now I realize that our existence at and after the Second Coming of Jesus will be far better than our current existence. So now I am not fearful when praying, "Thy Kingdom come". Actually, we don't have to wait for the Second Coming of Jesus for this part of the prayer to be answered. When we are fully immersed in our faith and invite Jesus to guide our thoughts, words, and deeds, or even to be our thoughts, words, and deeds, we are participating in God's Kingdom on earth. And one additional thought about this part is that if "Thy Kingdom come" is rephrased and converted into a question, specifically, How does God's Kingdom come?, it can be answered nicely by the next phrase in the prayer: Thy will be done on earth as it is in heaven.

When we pray "Thy will be done on earth as it is in heaven", we show respect for God and His authority. But it also is for our benefit that we pray this phrase. In no uncertain terms, God's will is what is best for us. In other words, there is no better way for us to live than by following His will. This is the only way for us to reach our utmost happiness, joy, inspiration, contentment, and peace.

I suspect that most of us have mixed feelings about the parts of the Lord's Prayer dealing with forgiveness (...and forgive us our trespasses, as we forgive those who trespass against us...). Undoubtedly, we like the idea of being forgiven, but do we like the idea of forgiving others? Probably not as much. In Matthew 6:15, Jesus says, "But if ye forgive men not their trespasses, neither will your Father forgive your trespasses."

God expects us to forgive others just as much as He wants to be able to forgive us, and probably more than we want and expect Him to forgive us. To be forgiven, we first need to humbly acknowledge our sins and to be sorry for them. And I think that holding onto our negative feelings for others, and withholding our forgiveness for them, creates negative baggage that gets in the way of the nourishing and strengthening of our faith. It is harmful to us and others.

"And lead us not into temptation" seems a little confusing. I agree with Luther, who says that God tempts no one. To me, this phrase is another way of saying "and lead us away from temptation" or "and give me the courage to avoid temptation".

Why do we need to ask for forgiveness?

Some people might tend to think that since Jesus died for the forgiveness of our sins, we don't need to acknowledge or confess our sins and ask for forgiveness anymore. They might think that we are already covered, so why do we need to bother with this extra nuisance (confession and asking for forgiveness)?

If we don't do these things as part of our faith, we are at risk of losing our faith. There is a downhill course that could result in the loss of our faith. We might start this downhill course by embracing the attitude that sin is OK, since Jesus has us covered anyway. Then we would progress to the idea that since sin is so much fun, it's better to sin even more. And, since Jesus has me covered anyway, I will simply be forgiven more. As we become more and more complacent in this downward spiral, we soon lose sight of what a tremendous thing that Jesus did for us. We begin to think, "Jesus? Oh, yeah, the forgiveness guy. He's got me covered, so I don't even have to think about sin." The next thing we know, we're thinking, "I'm going to stop thinking about Jesus since he already took care of my sin, whatever that is!" Finally, we forget to think of him at all. "Jesus? Who is that???"

If we include honest reflection on our own sinfulness and a request for forgiveness in our daily prayer(s), the value of what Jesus did for us stays strong in our minds and we are at much less risk of losing our faith. *Can't we ignore God's Law, since we have forgiveness available to us?*

In response to this question, Jesus tells us, "No." In Matthew 5:17 and 18, Jesus says, "Think not that I am come to destroy the law, or the prophets: I am not come to destroy, but to fulfil. For verily I say unto you, Till heaven and earth pass, one jot or one tittle shall in no wise pass from the law, till all be fulfilled."

In Mark 12:29–31, Jesus tells us what are the most important laws for us to know and keep: "The first of all commandments is, Hear, O Israel; The Lord our God is one Lord: And thou shalt love the Lord thy God with all thy heart, and with all thy soul, and with all thy mind, and with all thy strength: this is the first commandment. And the second is like, namely this, Thou shalt love thy neighbor as thyself. There is none other commandment greater than these."

I feel certain that God wants us to honor and to continue to follow the Ten Commandments as well. So, in terms of what laws to follow, I think that it is sufficient for us to follow what Jesus told us in Mark 12:29–31, plus the Ten Commandments. How else are we to know whether our actions are sinful if we don't know and try to follow God's commandments? Of course, the Holy Spirit helps us in this regard, but we can more easily understand the input we receive from the Holy Spirit if we already have the knowledge of the commandments given to us by Jesus along with the Ten Commandments.

My prayers

I like to think of my various prayers to God as intermittent parts of my ongoing conversation with God.

No believer in Jesus (which necessarily also means believer in God the Father and God the Holy Spirit) always has to pray exactly as other believers do. Jesus gave us the Lord's Prayer, which we should all use, but I think that most of our other prayers should be of our own creation, customized to our own lives and circumstances. I have included examples of my prayers to help explain my faith and beliefs rather than to tell you that you should pray as I do.

I do believe that we should not only pray for people inside of our own spheres of influence and interaction, but also outside of them. And we should not only pray for people whom we think favorably of, but we should also pray for those whom we don't hold in high regard, including people we perceive to be our enemies.

We should pray earnestly. If we don't pray with meaning and with our full attention, the prayer won't mean much to God, either. We shouldn't pray with the idea of just getting through the prayer; instead, our full attention should be devoted to each part of the prayer. I frequently struggle with this. My mind often gets distracted while I pray. Sometimes it gets distracted by thoughts connected to the prayer, but often gets distracted by earthly thoughts not related to the prayer. God understands our frailties and earthly interruptions while praying, and I am quite sure that He much prefers us to pray in an intermittent manner than not at all, so long as we are making a diligent effort to pray.

And we should pray truthfully. I have a souvenir tea mug (many would call it a coffee mug) that is covered with Mark Twain quotations. One is about prayer. Its words are, "You cannot pray a lie." How very true! (Well, maybe you can attempt to pray a lie, but it would be a worthless pursuit, as well as being disrespectful to God, and to yourself).

After experiencing "5:42", I became much more convinced of the power of prayer than I previously had been. And since starting this book, my appreciation for the power of prayer has increased even more. Since childhood I have been aware of stories of seemingly miraculous results from prayer. I confess that I was sometimes doubtful about these stories, but then I would remind myself that the Bible is filled with similar stories. If I believe in God (the Holy Trinity), I should not disregard such stories. I should not be skeptical at all regarding what God can do, since He is certainly not a lightweight, low-energy God! For God, everything is possible and nothing is impossible! So why not believe the miraculous sounding stories?! I now find these stories to be even more readily believable, and my skepticism continues to decrease.

As you will see, my daily prayer (or the prayer that I at least get partway through daily) has become fairly long. It started small and gradually grew to its current size. I try to go through this prayer while walking or bicycling; sometimes I go through short parts of it while driving, or cooking, or during various other activities, or "inactivities". My attention often shifts from the prayer to related thoughts about God. Sometimes I find my thoughts going where they shouldn't, and then I ask for forgiveness and try to refocus. I often experience pauses in my daily prayer due to interruption by other life events. Sometimes the pauses last several hours, but I usually have no trouble picking up where I left off.

You will see that I have phrases that I repeat at various points in my prayer. These phrases I call my "Joyful

Noises unto the Lord." The Bible tells us that we should "make a joyful noise unto the Lord." The number of times that I use such phrases varies from day to day. My oldest "joyful noise" phrase is my mother's favorite mealtime prayer; it's actually a combination prayer, the second part being from the book of Psalms). It goes as follows: Come Lord Jesus, be Thou our guest, let Thy (or these) gifts to us be blest. Oh, give thanks unto the Lord, for He is good, and His mercy endureth forever. Amen. More recently I have added this "joyful noise" phrase: O Lord, how great thou art, and how great your love for us is! Sometimes my "joyful noise" is even shorter, and may simply be: Oh, Yahoo! (one of my mom's favorite expressions) or Hallelujah!

I have other, much shorter prayers for various circumstances, such as getting the day started. I will record some of my shorter prayers for you also, but I will start with my daily prayer, which I think of as "The Big Prayer".

The Big Prayer

O Lord, God in Heaven and on earth, Father, Son, and Holy Spirit, how great Thou art, and how great Your love for us is! O Lord, God the Father, how great Thou art, and how great Your love for us is! Our Father, Who art in Heaven, hallowed be Thy Name, Thy Kingdom come, Thy Will be done on earth as it is in Heaven, give us this day our daily bread, and forgive us our trespasses, as we forgive those who trespass against us, and lead us not into temptation, but deliver us from evil, for Thine is the Kingdom, and the Power, and the Glory, forever and ever. Amen. How great Thou art, O Lord God our Heavenly Father, and how great Your love for us is!

O Lord God, our Lord and Savior Jesus Christ, how great Thou art, and how great your love for us is! O Lord

Jesus, You are the Son of God the Father, You are our Savior, our Redeemer! You did all of the following according to plan: You joined humanity on earth, incarnate. You taught us how to live, You taught us our faith, and You taught us the way to eternal life with You. You then suffered and died for us on the cross because of our sins and for our salvation. You then descended into hell, where you completed your suffering for our salvation. You then rose from the dead on the third day, thereby completing Your victory over death and damnation for us, so that we can be given the gifts of forgiveness of sins and eternal life with You. How great Thou art, Lord Jesus, and how great Your love for us is!

O Lord God, our Holy Spirit of God, how great Thou art, and how great your love for us is! O Holy Spirit of God, You proceed with love from the Father and the Son, and together with the Father and the Son You are worshipped and glorified. I don't understand You, but I often sense Your presence and Your love. You are our Holy connection, our Holy inspiration, our Holy guide, and our Holy comforter. How great Thou art, O Holy Spirit of God, and how great Your love for us is!

O Lord God, Father, Son, and Holy Spirit, how great Thou art, and how great your love for us is! You are eternal! Great is Your creation, Your power, Your love, Your mercy, Your grace, Your peace, Your forgiveness, Your sacrifice for us, Your inspiration for us, Your connection with us, Your guidance of us, Your comforting of us, Your patience with us, Your omnipotence, Your omniscience, Your holiness, and Your glory! You are far, far, far, far, far beyond my understanding. Please sustain me with Your love and with a simple, strong, and child-like faith!

O Lord, Father, Son, and Holy Spirit, I am full of sin and empty of good, or, if there is any good within me, it is as filthy rags. The list of my sins is long. Many are known to me and many are unknown to me. My sins are of thought, word, and deed, and sometimes of omission. Some are premeditated. Please have mercy on me and please forgive me. Please cleanse me. Please strengthen and guide me. Please help me to resist temptation and want to do so as well. Please help me to forgive others and want to do so as well. Please help me to live one day at a time according to Your Will and want to do so as well. Please have mercy on me and please forgive me. And Lord, please help me with my own self-righteousness each and every day.

O Lord, thank You for everything that you do for us and give to us. Especially thank You for the greatest of gifts that You give us, which include Yourself, the forgiveness of our sins, and eternal life with You! You give us these greatest of gifts if we believe in You (God the Father, God the Son, and God the Holy Spirit) and if we know that You, Lord Jesus, have already paid the price for our salvation, and if we know that we cannot attain salvation without our faith in You, Lord Jesus, and if we confess our sins and are sorry for them. Thank You, Lord, for these greatest of gifts, the extents of which are far beyond my understanding.

Hallelujah, come Lord Jesus, be Thou our guest, let Thy gifts to us be blest! O give thanks unto the Lord, for He is good, and His mercy endureth forever! Amen.

O Lord, please bless and keep my wife, my sons, my daughters-in-law, my grandchildren, and me. Please bless and keep those who are, or have been, or will be dear to any of us, as well as their families. Please bless and keep my wife's family and the families of my daughters-in-law. Please bless and keep my aunts, uncle, and cousins, and all of their families. Please bless and keep our extended families, our friends, neighbors, and coworkers, as well as their families. Please bless and keep those who are "downtrodden" (the homeless, those suffering from illness and other medical conditions, injury, mental health problems, and disabilities, those who suffer from hunger, thirst, poverty, or loneliness, those who suffer due to prejudice, discrimination, and hatred, as well as those who allow themselves to be filled with prejudice, discrimination, and hatred [please bless them by helping them to replace these things with Your love], those who are trapped by the bonds of slavery, human trafficking, sexual exploitation, and abusive relationships, those who are refugees, hostages, or in any other way suffering due to war, and those whom I have failed to mention). Please bless and keep those whom we call on for help with our spiritual and education needs, health and appearance needs, financial and home needs, and any and all of the rest of our needs and wants; please bless and keep their families as well. Please bless and keep everyone with whom I have ever attended church, and everyone with whom I went through any part of my education and training; please bless and keep their families as well. Please bless and keep all of my patients and their families. Please bless and keep everyone with whom I ever worked, as well as their families. Please bless and keep all of the medical professionals in the world, as well as their families. Please bless them with the knowledge that they have a wonderful opportunity in which to serve You and live their faith. Please bless and keep the people of the states and nations in which we or our sons and their families have lived, currently live, or will live. Please bless and keep all of Your children (all people) according to their needs, especially those who suffer heartache. Please bless everyone for whom I pray with strong doses of Your love and of the true faith in You (Father, Son, and Holy Spirit). May Your love and the true faith in You, O Lord, spread and flourish throughout the entire world. Please bless and keep us all, and protect us all from the evils, ills, and dangers of the world. Please help us to learn, know, love, and follow Your will, so that our faith is strengthened, so that we are better able to witness for You, so that we are better able to help each other, especially those less fortunate than ourselves, and so that we are better able to help the earth, as well.

O Lord, please bless and keep our leaders, our troops, our fire-fighters, our police men and women, and our public servants. Please bless them, protect them, guide them along Your path, and help them to be sure that they are on the right mission, causing no harm that they shouldn't be causing. Please guide our leaders along the path to peace and helpfulness for the people and for the earth. Please guide us and them away from war. Please help our leaders to get along, so that they are better able to help our country and the rest of the world. Please bless our President and Congress with wisdom, cooperation, compassion, courage, perseverance, and peace-seeking, so that they will be more able to help our country and the rest of the world. Please bless the world leaders in the same manner, and everywhere please replace bad leadership with good leadership, and bad leaders with good leaders, so that all leaders will be better able to help their own countries and the rest of the world. O Lord, there is such trouble on earth, such evil, hatred, and terrible warfare, such trouble within nations, including hatred and divisiveness, such destruction and devastation, such upheaval and forced migration, such suffering, heartache, and heartbreak, such disease, pestilence, and famine, and such poor treatment of the earth! O Lord, please have mercy on us! Please shower us with your love, and may we be filled with your love so that it overflows from our hearts and touches others whom we meet! Please help us to have peace and meaningful progress for Your children and for the earth! Please have mercy on us! And Lord, for You everything is possible and nothing is impossible! Please magnify my little prayer into big results for Your children and Your kingdom!..... And please bless all of us who believe in You with the certainty that You will ultimately bless us in a much better way!

Hallelujah, come Lord Jesus, be Thou our guest, let Thy gifts to us be blest. O give thanks unto the Lord, for He is good, and His mercy endureth forever! Amen.

O Lord, please bless all of Your children who are engaged in honest employment. Please help them to do the best they can in their jobs or professions, according to Your will. Please help Your children who are seeking employment to find employment in which they can thrive, according to Your will. And please bless those who are engaged in dishonest, evil activities by overwhelming them with Your love and inspiration so that they know that they must replace their evil ways with Your good ways. Please continue to bless them as they do this. Please help all of Your children, including those already mentioned, as well as babies, young children, students, retirees, and those in any other category, to be able do the best they can, in all aspects of their lives, according to Your will.

Please thwart those who want to harm or kill others because they think that somehow these actions honor You, or their version of You. Please also thwart those who want to harm or kill others, without having any thoughts of honoring You, or anyone's version of You. Please thwart them all, here and abroad, now and in the future, and please help them learn the true way to love and honor You. And if they learn the true way to love and honor You, and actually do it, please continue to bless them in all sorts of good ways! Please make them shining examples to help bring many more people to the true faith in You, O Lord!

O Lord, almost wherever anyone looks on earth there is war, or the threat of war, or some other trouble. Please help us to give up our evil, sinful, violent, destructive, prideful, and selfish ways, and to replace them with Your good ways. Please help us to learn to love and respect each other, and to take better care of each other. And please help us to learn to respect the earth, and to remember that it is your creation not only for us, but for all of your creatures.

Please help those who are struggling to overcome the effects of natural disasters and human-caused disasters. Please inspire us to help them as well. And please give us the wisdom and resolve to better prepare, and save, for future disasters.

O Lord, please help and bless the drought-stricken areas, the flood-damaged and storm-damaged areas, and all famine relief efforts. Please help the climate to moderate and improve. Please help us learn to take much better care of the earth, and to actually do it. Please bless the firefighters who are battling wildfires; please bless them with safety, and with rain and favorable weather when and where needed, according to Your Will. We do not deserve Your blessings and mercies, but we depend on them. Please have mercy on us!

O Lord, thank You for the many blessings that You have given me, blessings that I don't deserve and for which I am not always thankful, blessings which I often take for granted, and blessings with which I am sometimes dissatisfied. Please forgive me for my sinfulness regarding Your blessings to me. Please help me to always cherish the gifts that I should cherish, especially my wife, sons, daughters-in-law, and grandchildren. Please help me to cherish all of Your children in the manner that You want me to. And please help me to use wisely those gifts that I should use wisely.

Please help more people to be in Your fold and stay in Your fold. Please help everyone for whom I pray to be in Your fold and stay in Your fold. Please help as many as possible to be in Your fold and stay in Your fold.

Please help us to remember to call on You not only in times of trouble, but also when there is no trouble in our lives. Please help us to remember that we should call on You at all times, O Lord!

Please always be with my family and me, and please help us to always be with You. Please always be with everyone for whom I pray, and please help all of us to always be with You!

In Jesus' Name I pray, Amen!

Hallelujah, come Lord Jesus, be Thou our guest, let Thy gifts to us be blest. O give thanks unto the Lord, for He is good, and His mercy endureth forever. Halleluiah! Oh, Yahoo! and Amen!

A Prayer to Start the Day

O Lord God, Father, Son, and Holy Spirit, how great Thou art, and how great Your love for us is! Good morning to You, Lord! Thank You for this day that You have created for us! Please be with us today and please help us be with You today. In Jesus' Name I pray, Amen!

A Prayer for Courage, Wisdom, Strength, Humility, and Love

O Lord, please bless me with the necessary courage, wisdom, strength, humility, and love to follow Your Will and to follow the inspiration that You give me. Please be with me always, and please help me to always be with You. In Jesus' Name I pray, Amen.

A Prayer to Divert My Mind from Evil, Angry, or Otherwise Negative Thoughts

(You may recognize this prayer from church services or from reading the Bible [Psalm 51]. Sometimes this is helpful after thinking it one time, but sometimes I have to repeat this a few times, with increased focus, for it to be helpful).

Create in me a clean heart, O God, and renew a right spirit within me. Cast me not away from Your presence, and take not your Holy Spirit from me. Restore to me the joy of Your salvation, and uphold me with Thy Free Spirit. Amen.

My Going to Work Prayer

(As you might suspect, I no longer use this prayer. Anyone can modify this prayer to fit their work circumstances).

O Lord, please be with me at work tonight, and please help me to be with You. Please give me the wisdom, strength and knowledge to do my job, according to Your will. Please help me to do the best that I can, according to Your will. Please help me to be positive, and not whine and complain. Please help me to be eager, thankful, and happy to work, and to be a good example to my coworkers, patients, and their families. Please help me to remember that all of my patients and their families, and all of my coworkers are Your children, and that all should be treated with kindness and respect. Please help me to remember to call on You in times of trouble, and even when there is no trouble; I should call on You at all times, O Lord! In Jesus' Name I pray, Amen.

A Prayer Before Reading the Bible

O Lord, thank You for the gift of the Bible. Please help me to always remember that this gift to us contains the Words of Eternal Life! Please be with me and inspire me as I read Your Word. Please help me to see and understand Your wisdom. Please help me to see and appreciate how Your Word absolutely has meaning for me and the present world. In Jesus' Name I pray, Amen.

A Prayer of Thankfulness for the Beauty of God's Creation

O Lord, thank You for the absolutely beautiful day (and/or absolutely beautiful earth) that You have created for us and have blessed us with! Thank You! Thank You! Thank You! Oh, Yahoo! and Amen.

One more thing on prayer. Don't be discouraged if you never have a prayer that is so definitely and immediately answered like mine in the "5:42" story. That has only happened once to me, that I know of. And I don't think that you can just casually decide to pray like that and expect an answer like I received. I don't think that I had ever before prayed with as much spontaneous feeling as I did then. I do think that God answers prayers very frequently, but the answers are usually not very obvious to us because they are woven into the fabric of our daily lives, so to speak. The answers to our prayers are often in the form of people we encounter and our interactions with them.

Finally, I will try to remember to pray for you, and would you please pray for me?! Oh, Yahoo! and Amen.

Looking for a sign?

A few months ago, I found a great message in the men's room of one of my favorite restaurants. I suspect that you're already skeptical. What message could I possibly find in the men's room that is suitable for printing here?

I won't make you wait too much longer. It wasn't scrawled on the stall wall, as most men's room messages are; rather, it was printed on a sign hanging on the wall beside the door. It was meant to be seen upon exiting. It read, "If you're looking for a sign, this is it." (Or, it may have read, "If you're looking for a sign, here it is"). I chuckled out loud and thought, "What a great message!" It made me laugh, but it also made me think. I told our friends about it, and they also laughed. So, it was more effective than a lot of restroom messages. And it reminded me a little of my favorite poem, one that I learned many years ago from Johnny Carson (Roses are red, violets are blue, some poems rhyme, but this one doesn't).

With a little imagination, you can find some meaning in the message, maybe lots. It probably can be applied to lots of situations.

When I first thought that it might be useful for this book, I was thinking in terms of the following. "If you're looking for a sign, I hope that what I have written is in some small, medium, or large way the sign that you have been looking for." Now, I simply will say, "If you're looking for a sign, look no farther than the Bible, for it contains the most powerful words ever written, the Words of Eternal Life!"

Science and Related Topics

The value of science

For me, and probably for many others, there are connections between science and our faith. Still others see no connection between science and our faith. I'm okay with that, and I'm pretty sure that God is also okay with that. What I write here is not necessary for our faith or salvation. I am writing to show that these connections help me to understand my faith and beliefs, and that there isn't a problem with connecting science and our faith. I will try to shed some light on these connections, as I see them. This may be helpful to people who don't fully embrace their faith because they sense or have been told that it is at odds with science.

Staying Current with Science News Magazine

In the early 1990s, I started regularly reading the publication *Science News Magazine*. I had seen an issue at my parents' house and it looked interesting. I thought that since I'm in a science-related profession, I should keep up with what is going on in other areas of science. The magazine looked manageable for me to read.

It took a little discipline for me to read each issue, but once I would get started, it wasn't hard to finish. I found the articles interesting. As I learned about more and more scientific discoveries, I began to reflect on these discoveries, especially when I had more time to reflect. I found that the best time to reflect was when I was on a two to three-hour bicycle ride. More and more, with adequate time to reflect on it, I could see how awesome God's creation is. The sheer complexity of life especially fascinated me.

I started to view my reading of *Science News Magazine* as a type of religious experience. It seemed to reinforce my beliefs.

Pertinent to the complexity of life, I was awed by the information in an article in Science News on DNA (September 5, 2015 issue — The human genome takes shape and shifts over time, by Sarah Schwarz). Vastly more is known now about DNA than when I was in medical school about forty years ago. But it seems that the more we learn about DNA, the more obvious it is that we have a long way to go to fully understand it. Now it appears that DNA is a very complex computer housed within a very complex machine, or a blend of the two. It contains its own very complex instructions for developing all of the cell types in the body (or in whatever organism the DNA is from), instructions for organizing the cells into different types of organs, instructions for cell migration, instructions for folding itself into extremely compact bundles that have amazingly sophisticated arrangements despite their extremely compact nature, instructions for unfolding, instructions for rearranging its configuration depending on the cell's needs, etc., etc.,........And all of these bundles of computer/machines fit snugly into an extremely small nucleus. And this is a very simple description of DNA; I have left out many features and functions of DNA. It is mind-boggling, at least to me, to imagine that DNA could develop without divine influence! To me, DNA is the signature of God in the all of the various life forms that He created! I read elsewhere that Bill Gates commented on DNA, saying, "DNA is like a computer program, but far, far more advanced than any software ever created."

The more I read about scientific discoveries, the more awe I have for the beyond-amazing and beyond-description knowledge, power, and capabilities of our God!

Creation and evolution

In my earlier years, I believed what the church taught, that we were created and that there was no place for evolution in our beliefs. But as I learned more science, I would increasingly think that there is good evidence for evolution. This would lead to conflicts in my mind. I knew that God existed and that the Bible says that He created everything. How was I to assimilate my increasing respect for the evidence of evolution? This conflict simmered for many years. I would tend to file it away in some less conspicuous part of my mind, but occasionally it would boil over a little and require that I revisit it. I would also revisit it when I periodically learned about conflicts between the proponents of creationism and those supporting evolution in relation to school curricula.

One particular thought which ultimately helped me resolve this simmering conflict concerns the way that God regards time. Second Peter, 3:8 says, "But, beloved, be not ignorant of this one thing, that with the Lord one day is as a thousand years, and a thousand years as one day." I remember hearing this as a child (Of course, I didn't remember where it said this in the Bible). It was confusing to me then, but as an adult I began to think that if one day is as a thousand years, it probably is also as a million years or even a billion years, or any number of years. That led to me thinking about the creation story in the Bible. The "days" of creation likely could be interchanged with billions of years, or anything between the two. I think that Peter speaks of a thousand years instead of a million or billion because people probably didn't think in terms of millions or billions when he wrote the verse I mentioned earlier; a thousand was more comprehensible.

The creation story in the Bible doesn't tell us the details of how God was able to create. There was no need to. The details would have been far too complex for people to understand, especially before we had much scientific knowledge. And even today we don't have enough scientific knowledge to understand very much of how God created. From a human perspective, we have a lot of scientific knowledge, but we know also that there is vastly more to learn. I suspect that from God's perspective, our scientific knowledge is still in a fetal stage. Anyway, I think that the creation story was kept simple for our sake. The choice of using days vs. billions of years in the story was accurate for God because God operates outside of time. And when we take into account Second Peter, 3:8, the choice to use days in the creation story can be accurate for us, also, even if we think that the story played out over a much longer period of time, according to our understanding of time.

All of this ultimately led me to wonder whether there is even a conflict between evolution and creation. If one thinks of evolution (the innate ability of life to evolve) as one of God's wondrous creations, then there is NO conflict between creation and evolution. The only conflict between the two seems to be in our imaginations.

I don't pretend to know how God created, but I do think that He did create the means for evolution and incorporated this into all of the various life forms. The means of evolution lies within DNA. I have read of strong evidence for evolutionary changes occurring in a single species in the animal kingdom in as little as forty years. However, in viruses, evolutionary changes can be seen within weeks, and probably much faster than that. And there is more than enough evidence for evolution over the long term (hundreds of millions of years, or more). It is my belief that evolution operates according to God's plans and is not the result of strictly chance occurrences. I think that God didn't tell us about it because there was no need for us to know; it has nothing to do with our path to salvation. I don't think that He was or is trying to deceive us by withholding information on how He created; rather, I imagine him telling us something like the following: "If you needed to know about evolution, I would have revealed it to you in the Bible. But, if you insist on knowing, look at the evidence and figure it out, and don't forget Who did the creating and got all of this started!"

Why would God create the means for evolution? While I certainly don't know God's reasons for this, I can imagine at least two possibilities. He knew that the earth would have changing conditions, and a means of evolution would help His creatures adapt to changing conditions. And I think that it would be more interesting to God to be able to watch His creation change and adapt, or, in other words, evolve. And there might have been another purpose for evolution, one that I wouldn't have considered mentioning had I written this book forty or more years ago. And what is that purpose? To create humans.... What?!! That's contrary to the Bible!....Well, I'm not sure that it is. I will address my thoughts on this in what follows.

Did man evolve, was he created, or was it both?

I think it was both. How did I arrive at this thought? Part of the answer is in what you have just read and the rest is as follows.

I will start with basketball, of course! I have always loved basketball since learning about it in grade school. I was never good at it, but maybe that is partly why I love watching the game so much; I have always had an appreciation for the skill and agility of good basketball players. And since childhood I have been a fan of the University of Nebraska men's basketball team. I'm what you might call a die-hard fan, because my team has never attained the level of success that I desire for them.

Nebraska's coach from 2000 until 2006 was Barry Collier, a man whom I admired greatly. I thought that he was a good coach and was disappointed when I learned that he was fired (for not attaining the desired level of success). One of my fondest memories of him was learning that he was a prolific reader of the Bible. I remember him saying that he had read the Bible about five or six times. I was impressed. With each reading, he said that he learned lots of new things he hadn't noticed or understood before. This was inspirational to me. I thought that I had better get started! At that point, I hadn't read much of the Old Testament, and had never read much of the New Testament beyond the Gospels.

Around 2003, I started reading the Bible regularly. My plan was to read a chapter of the Old Testament every day and a chapter of the New Testament every day. On average, I probably read three to four days per week (I have slacked on this pace since then, but occasionally read several chapters in one day). My Bible reading often took place between 2 AM and 4 AM, when I was in what I called "night mode", a side effect of working a varied schedule in the E.R.

Almost right away I found something in the Bible that really got my attention. The creation story in Genesis 1:27 and 28 says, "So God created man in his own image, in the image of God created He him; male and female created He them. And God blessed them, and God said unto them, be fruitful and multiply, and replenish the earth, and subdue it............" The last verse in chapter 1 says that this occurred on the sixth day.

Genesis Chapter 2:1 says, "Thus the heavens and the earth were finished, and all the host of them." Verse 2 says, "And on the seventh day God ended His work which He had made....." The end of verse 5 says, "and there was not a man to till the ground." Verse 7 says, "And the Lord God formed man of the dust of the ground, and breathed into his nostrils the breath of life, and man became a living soul." Verse 7 referred to the creation of the man who was first referred to as Adam in verse 19. Verse 21 and 22 relate the story of the creation of Eve, although her name doesn't appear until chapter 3:20.

The next verses of significance in this line of thought are chapter 4:15–17, which say, "......And the Lord set a mark upon Cain, lest any finding him should kill him. And Cain went out from the presence of the Lord, and dwelt in the land of Nod, on the east of Eden. And Cain knew his wife; and she conceived..."

When I read and reread these verses (many times, to make sure that my thoughts were reasonable), I thought, "Is the Bible telling me that the human race was established before the creation of Adam and Eve?" We are not told that Adam and Eve are the people that were created on the sixth day. Were Adam and Eve created to start the line of people who would lead to Jesus? The Bible does outline the connection between Adam and Eve and Jesus. Was this line of people created also to initiate agriculture (...and there was not a man to till the ground...); was there no agriculture until Adam or Cain? Were all of the people who may have existed before Adam's creation hunter-gatherers? If Cain's wife wasn't his sister, and there is no mention of his wife being his sister, and no mention of a sister at all, then his wife came from another line of people, possibly a line of people that had evolved.

All of this boils down to the question of whether it was incest or evolution that played a major role in the start of the human race. I suspect that God isn't a big fan of incest, so I can't help but think it was evolution. And in regard to "the Lord setting a mark upon Cain, lest any finding him should kill him", who was it that would find Cain and kill him? His siblings, or some other people already present on earth?

Recently, I researched whether anyone else has written anything like these thoughts I have had for about thirteen years. I found that Rev. Jim Persinger had thoughts that overlap considerably with mine; I think his article was posted about eleven years ago. While I didn't search further, I suspect that many people in the past have had these same thoughts but have likely kept quiet about them for fear of being accused of heresy or blasphemy.

In 1 Corinthians 15:45, Paul refers to the first man, Adam (he doesn't specify whether Adam was the first man [period!], or the first man in the paternal line of Jesus). So I can see that many, possibly most, will continue to stick with the traditional interpretation, which I think is okay. This is something that doesn't matter for salvation. Maybe we can all find out the correct version in Heaven!

Several weeks after recording the thoughts above, the following thoughts on the creation of Adam and Eve came to me. I have left my earlier thoughts in place so that you can see the evolution of my thoughts. One new thought, which is probably rather elementary to many theologians and pastors, is that Adam and Eve may have been created by God so that He could directly introduce Himself to the human race. Adam and Eve would have been perfect and sin-free until they became polluted by sin due to the wiles of Satan. When they were in their perfect state, they would have been able to be in the presence of God. I think that God knew from the moment of creation that Adam and Eve would fall into a sinful state, and if there were people who preceded Adam and Eve, they were undoubtedly already in a sinful state. When we are in a sinful state, we are not able to be in the presence of God. God knew that in order to introduce Himself to the human race, this had to be accomplished with perfect humans, before they fell into sin (enter Adam and Eve).

And why would God need to introduce himself to humans? To lay the groundwork, or foundation, of His plan for our salvation! One part of this foundation is that we must have knowledge of good and evil! If people preceded Adam and Eve, and if they were sinful (which undoubtedly they were), they wouldn't have known they were sinful until after Adam and Eve acquired the knowledge of good and evil in the Garden of Eden.

Another thought I have had regarding Adam and Eve concerns genetics. God likely wanted the descendants of Adam and Eve to be genetically robust because He needed them for the further progression of His plan of salvation. Genetics comes into play because it would be easier to keep the line of Adam and Eve's descendants genetically robust if genetically diverse human "stock" was available for them to blend with (i.e., humans who had been created through the mechanisms of evolution). Otherwise, God would likely have had to do a lot of corrective tinkering with their DNA for many generations, something of course that He would have been more than capable of doing.

It may or may not have happened this way. God did not give us the details of how we were created. I think that for those of us who value science, and may sense, as I do, that science reflects on the magnificence of God's creation, this is a way that helps reconcile perceived differences between faith and science.

What are we to make of the evidence?

If all of the fossilized remains of ancient life forms that have been discovered don't represent evidence for evolution, then what do they represent? Was God simply practicing His creative skills without intending for us to discover the evidence of His practice rounds of creation? I don't think so. Did He create the fossils to provide us a test of our faith? I don't think so. If this were the case, I'm sure that He would have given us clues about it in the Bible. God is certainly more than capable of giving us the information we need – if we are willing to "search the scriptures." Did Satan create the fossils to try to deceive us? I don't think so. If the Bible says that Satan has this type of creative ability, I certainly missed it. Should we accept that all of the fossilized remains are from evolution caused by random events? This explanation doesn't work for me because I know that God exists and He has told us that He is the Creator. While I suspect that it also doesn't work for the rest of us who believe in God, I can see this answer working for people who don't believe in God........ I see no problem with just going with, or accepting, the idea that evolution is part of God's creation. I think that evolution is simply a very "creative" way of creating, devised by our very smart God!

I believe that God intentionally kept information in the Bible supporting evolution obscure. Had it been more obvious, many more readers of the Bible may have been confused by it long before we knew about evolution.

A new approach is warranted (for some of us)

Let me begin by saying that I don't think God requires us to choose which version of the creation story to believe – the traditional one taught for thousands of years, or a version that includes evolution as one of God's magnificent creative mechanisms. I have not seen anywhere in the Bible that this decision and belief is necessary for our salvation.

To the proponents of the traditional approach, please be careful to not insist that believing in the traditional creation story is necessary for a person's salvation. This approach may keep some people who see and understand the strong evidence for evolution from ever wanting to explore our faith. You do not want to be responsible for being a detriment to their faith development!

If you are inclined to share my opinion on this issue, also please do not insist that others have to agree with you. We should not place stumbling blocks on anyone's path to faith development, regardless of what our belief is regarding creation with or without evolution!

Physics of faith (and a little chemistry and math)

While on a bike ride about a year after retirement, I began thinking about God's plan of salvation, and how it differed from the plans that we would devise, if we had the power to do so. I remember thinking, "It's a great plan, but why did God choose the plan that He did (see Faith Prescription or My Prayers for the basics of His plan). This led me to think that there must be some basic, underlying reason why it has to be this way, a reason not known to us.

Our world operates in accordance with a number of natural laws. Could it be that this type of governance also applies to the supernatural realm (God, Heaven, Hell, Faith, Forgiveness, Good vs. Evil, etc.)?

Getting back to God's plan of salvation, I wondered if there is some way to gauge the amount of forgiveness needed by each of us. Is it "one size fits all", or something other than that? Is forgiveness more than symbolic? Can it be quantified (not by us, but by God)? Are there units of forgiveness, or quanta of forgiveness? Is the reason for God's plan of salvation simply that we are incapable of being good enough, because of some basic law or laws of "supernature", to attain our own salvation? Perhaps only God, as human through Jesus, was able to endure the extent of suffering needed to cancel our debts from sin and evil. If Jesus was just human and not God, I suspect He wouldn't have been able to endure the extent of suffering needed for the task that He would accomplish.

And can forgiveness be stored for later use? Is it a form of energy that can be stored in something like a battery, or perhaps, in a battery within the "mind" of God? Or is there a currency of forgiveness, one in which units of that currency can be stored in accounts within God's "mind"?

How is forgiveness transmitted to us? Did God the Father know exactly how much suffering Jesus needed to endure so that all believers would be forgiven? Does our inability to attain salvation by our own means have to do with our sin-stained souls being unable to be cleansed by a sin-stained person? (Incidentally, this is the chemistry part. To me, it seems that self-cleaning attempts by a sin-stained person would still leave lots of stains. Isaiah's thoughts, found in Isaiah 64:6, help to explain this idea. He says, "But we are all as an unclean thing, and all of our righteousnesses are as filthy rags..." As you can imagine, one can't do a very good job cleaning with a filthy rag). The list of questions one could ask along these lines is practically endless...

If some of these seem like stupid questions, you might be right. And as you can see, I mostly have questions and only one or two attempts at answers. Deciding what the questions should be is difficult enough. That said, I have the feeling that the reason God the Father chose the plan of salvation that He did has something to do with "supernatural" laws of creation, laws that He created, laws that are understood only by Him. I suspect that Jesus' suffering and our forgiveness may be more than just symbolic. They may be quantifiable, but only to God. I think that because of these supernatural laws, created by God the Father, the only one able to do the required suffering was Jesus, the Son of God.

Another "physics of faith" topic, also with no real answers, concerns good and evil. This is where "math of faith" makes its appearance. It seems to me that if God's creation was derived from nothing, for there to be good, there also has to be evil, and there also has to be a balance between good and evil. Of course, I can only speculate in this regard, but simple math helps me to grasp at understanding this. Nothing = 0. Any amount of good, represented by a positive number, would have to be matched by a negative number of equal magnitude, representing a commensurate amount of evil, for the sum of the two to equal zero (nothing). For example, 1–1=0, or 2–2=0, and so on...I may be missing something, or a lot, but this just seems intuitive to me. It is likely more complicated than that, but this may be a way for us mere mortals to try to understand it.

The next consideration is that if God is the "champion" of good, there has to be a "champion" of evil. Of course, the "champion" of evil is Satan.

Then comes the thought, how does this thinking relate to the story of Satan (Lucifer) and his followers being expelled from heaven? Somehow, God managed to accomplish what I think of as the first great separation of good and evil (the second will start with the second coming of Jesus). Somehow, all of the good force(s) went to the side of God and His followers, and all of the evil force(s) went to the side of Satan and His followers. The moment that this separation was finalized may have occurred simultaneously with the expulsion of Satan and his followers from heaven.

The conflict between good and evil on earth has been playing out since creation. I believe that no one (human) is purely evil and no one is entirely good. Evil dwells in all of us. The battle between good and evil includes smaller battles raging subtly within each of us. Since we are polluted with evil, the good within us is like "filthy rags". That is why we all need God's forgiveness and His plan of salvation, the price of which Jesus has already paid!

We often forget, and some of us never knew, that we have the power to improve the outcome of our own share of the battle between good and evil. We do this by praying to God for help in this battle. As we learn to empower our prayers, increasingly more of God's love and more of God's power are available to us.

Prayer is another part of our faith practice that I suspect has connections to the realm of "physics of faith." A few things come to mind in this regard. By what mechanisms is prayer transmitted to God, and how does God communicate with us? Does God use quantum entanglement[2] for this purpose, or for transmitting forgiveness? Can the power of a prayer be measured by God, and are there units of prayer strength, known to God? This may have something to do with "miracles" occurring our world. If one's faith is strong enough, or if the combined faith of many is strong enough, the power of God can be unleashed for us to witness and benefit from. I will stop here. You can work out further details, or more questions, if you want to. You're now at least as good as I am at this exercise!

One can go on and on with potential "physics of faith" questions? Such as, is Heaven very near us, but we cannot sense it because it is in another dimension? Or, does dark matter have anything to do with Heaven? And so on and so on…

Maybe the answers to my "physics of faith" questions will be revealed in Heaven, or maybe my soul, once it detaches from my human mind and body, won't be concerned about such things.

---

[2] I won't attempt to explain this concept, but Einstein described it as "spooky action at a distance". A wealth of information online can be found by those who are interested.

Time

About ten to twelve years ago I listened to a series of recorded lectures on St. Augustine's Confessions, a book I have never read but hope to someday. While all of the lectures were interesting, I was especially excited to learn that Augustine, like me, had wrestled with understanding the concept of time, and that we share many of the same thoughts.

I have continued to periodically think of time. It is hard for us to imagine a world without time. It seems to be hardwired into us. I believe that God invented time to help manage His creation. Probably everything that we can think of in our world has some connection to time. This is especially evident in living things, but nonliving things also have connections to time-dependent cycles and changes. There are countless time-dependent cycles within cells and within systems in an organism; still other time-dependent cycles govern the organism as a whole. I believe that time-dependent cycles extend to all levels in the world and throughout the universe.

I think that there is no need for time in Heaven, except in regard to God and His staff watching over His creation.[3] God fully understands time since He created it. I imagine that it is infinitely easier for Him to know what will occur at any time in the future and to know what occurred at any time in the past than it is for us to remember what just happened a minute ago. Maybe the hard-to-understand concept of space-time has

---

[3] Regarding my personal experience with Marvin's death (see 'Unusual occurrences'), I am certain that "5:42" was information from God that was transmitted to me, so it is obvious to me that God is fully aware of all possible aspects of time on earth, even including time zones.

something to do with God's ease of knowing what happened in the past and what will happen in the future. God may think of time as we would think of navigating a terrain, but, of course, such navigation would be infinitely easier for God.

I wrote the thoughts above two months before writing what follows. It finally occurred to me that time may simply be an illusion. It may be that God's creation is so well interconnected, with countless perfectly interconnected cycles, and even some noncyclic series of events that are built from cyclic events, that all of life has the basic illusory understanding of time built into it.

Evolution may be an example of a noncyclic series of events (changes) built from countless cyclic events. The cyclic events would be those found within DNA, within cells, within organs, within organisms, within populations, and within all of life, and all of these cyclic events would be interacting with cyclic events outside of life but within the environment of life.

I like to think of time and God's perfect creation together in terms of flawless "clockwork", with the interconnectedness and extent of the "clockwork" being beyond our comprehension. God's creation is so perfect that all parts work together as a complex "clockwork" leading to the illusion of time. In other words, the concept of time itself may simply be a side effect of a perfect creation. We can't measure time except by measuring cyclic events; for example, our measurement of time, for most purposes, is based on measurements of the cyclic events within our solar system. If there were no cyclic events, time would become vastly different from the version of time that we currently "know".

Separating ourselves from time is currently impossible for us, but once we enter the realm of eternity, it will be easy.

Public Life

Government and politics

I have included these topics in my stories of faith because I think that they overlap with our faith and beliefs. We strive to have separation of church and state, but this is often difficult, especially in our minds.

First, I will address government. God values government. He is not antigovernment. He knows that all of us need the order and stability provided by government. Here is a well-known Bible verse that touches on the subject of government; Mark 12:17 says, "And Jesus answering said unto them, 'Render unto Caesar what is Caesar's, and render unto God what is God's.'" For more insight into this answer by Jesus, please read the first 16 verses of Mark, chapter 12. The entire chapter of Romans 13 has several interesting things to say about government and how we are to live within the framework provided by government.

Politics is a little messier to deal with than government, but obviously there is much overlap between the two. In this part, I will comment on a few issues that are political, or, at least, said to be political.

Immigration

I suspect that if one were to ask Native Americans about illegal immigrants, a lot of them would say that the rest of us are illegal immigrants. Or, maybe they would cut the African Americans some slack, since they were brought to America against their will.

Regarding different treatment for Muslims than for other groups of people, don't we still have freedom of religion here? It seems that most of us who are rallying against Muslims are supposedly Christians. For those of us who consider ourselves Christians, we must remember that

Jesus commanded us to love one another. He didn't tell us to just love those that look like us or worship as we worship. He was referring to all people being the recipients of our love when He told us to love one another. If we withhold our love from anyone, we are also withholding our love from Jesus. And when we withhold our love from anyone, we are followers of Satan and not Jesus. Another point regarding different treatment for Muslims is that if we treat them any differently from the rest of our population, this will only serve to inflame the few who are inclined to take matters outside of the law. The Bible tells us that God doesn't show partiality; Romans 2:11 says, "For there is no respect of persons with God." If this works for God, it should work for us, also.

Abortion

Until recently, I never thought that I would ever write about abortion. What good would it do? Very few minds are ever changed by writing or speaking on this topic. But since I have been trying a little harder recently to get into "what would Jesus do?" mode, I thought that I would see where connecting the two would take me. After lots of thought and a little prayer, I have arrived at the following point of view. I think Jesus would have a problem with the majority of those on both sides of the issue. I think that He might borrow a phrase from Dr. Phil and ask the pro-life people this, "How is that working for you? Or, more to the point, how is that working for the little ones and their moms?" He would point out that their approach isn't working. He would say that a new approach is needed, one that is more helpful, not only for the little ones, but also for their moms.

What would this approach be like? First, it would have to be a nonjudgmental approach, because we, as humans, aren't very qualified to judge each other. We have not walked in each other's footsteps. Each side would have to sincerely try to understand those on the other side of the issue. Those opposed to abortion would have to realize that those who seek abortion have most likely endured much more difficult life circumstances than they have. Many of those seeking abortions are suffering from emotional, financial, and relationship deprivations. They feel "at the end of their rope", or, "I'm damned if I do and damned if I don't, and, right now, damned if I do looks and feels a lot better than damned if I don't." Some see that abortion is legal, so it must be okay. And they probably don't share the same views about abortion as the pro-life people. They probably don't believe that a child is being killed with abortion, but, if they do, they feel that they are in that "damned if I do, damned if I don't situation", as already mentioned. On the other side of the issue, pro-choice people should try to understand that pro-life people absolutely believe that taking the life of a fetus is no different from intentionally killing a healthy baby already outside of the uterus. So, how far does that get us toward a solution? Not too far, I suspect.

The next step is to realize that this isn't really a political issue. Years ago, I heard something like that and thought, "How could it not be a political issue?" Now I think that I might understand. That it is not a political issue has to do with this question: What would be solved if there was a federal law making abortions illegal? If there was such a law, I think that the number of abortions would likely stay about the same. What?!!! I think that they would be done under a different name, or under the names of a number of different diagnostic or therapeutic procedures, to replace the name "abortion." And I think that many would be driven "underground", or out of the country. The pro-life people might congratulate themselves, thinking that they had accomplished something with such a law in place, while the actual numbers of abortions would likely be about the same; abortions would just have new names, or be done in new places.

So, is there a solution at all, and, if so, what would it look like? I have in mind a potential solution, a solution that I think might be a "what would Jesus do?" solution. I admit that most people would think that I am crazy for even trying to come up with a solution of any sort. And I admit that this would be costly, both financially and logistically. But a good share of it could be easily paid for if some well-meaning people redirected their donations to a worthy cause, such as this, instead of flushing them down the toilet and into the sewers of negative political advertising. They could even have short commercials for candidates that say, "So and so is donating this much money to the St. Lo Anthem (Save The Little Ones ANd help THEir Moms) Program Fund in support of candidate blankety-blank." This could be preceded and followed by a few seconds of peace and tranquility, in the form of pleasant music accompanying videos of pleasant scenes.

The heart of my plan is that women who are seeking an abortion could be given information on, and directed to, the St. Lo Anthem Program. This program, administered by a charitable organization or church, would provide helpers and other needed support, including financial support, to the women. In effect, the women would be relieved of their burdens that have contributed to them wanting abortions. They could stay at home and finish their pregnancy in peace, with helpers to help take care of the other children, if there are any, or to just be available for companionship and emotional support. Or, all of this could be done in the homes of wonderfully motivated people who want to help reduce abortions. Or, this could be done in a dormitory-like setting, with a sufficient and nonjudgmental staff present. The Catholic Church probably has the infrastructure and personnel to help with a project like this. And some other churches possibly do as well. And heaven knows that there is more than enough money that is currently being wasted that would fund such a program. This type of support would ideally remain in place for the women at least until a few weeks after delivery, to make sure everybody's needs are being met. Upon delivery, or shortly thereafter, the mom could decide if she is keeping the baby or putting the baby up for adoption.

Some might argue against this by saying, "It wouldn't work. People would scam the program." Of course they would! So what?! The people taking undue advantage of the program would be exposed to a level of human kindness that they probably didn't know was possible, and that might pay off spiritually and otherwise for them in the future. And the money would have been utterly wasted anyway if it were to have gone to political ads (which are really just another form of scamming) instead of to this program.

One thing that would be absolutely necessary for this to work is that it would have to entirely be a "what would Jesus do" endeavor. There would be no place for judgmental, holier-than-thou attitudes in the program's staff. That type of attitude would undoubtedly poison the program!

So, is this program, or a better version of it, actually workable? Yes, provided that enough people, or the right people, decide that the current standoff between pro-life and pro-choice proponents is absolutely not working for the little ones and their moms. If pro-life people aren't willing to consider something beyond the current standoff, are they really interested in helping the little ones, and their moms? And if pro-choice people aren't also willing to consider something like this, are they really interested in helping the women to the fullest extent possible? I suspect that there are many pro-choice people who would actually welcome a program like this.

For those of us who want to work through government channels to reduce abortion rates, regardless of whether we consider ourselves pro-life, pro-choice, or something in between the two, I absolutely recommend reading, with an open mind, Sam Corey's article entitled "3 Ways To Lower Abortion Rates That Are More Effective Than Closing Clinics."[*] This was published in Elite Daily, Politics. There is very good evidence that banning abortions doesn't reduce the rate of abortions. Improving economic conditions for mothers does help significantly, and one especially helpful way to do this is to provide paid maternity leave. And I suspect that paid family leave for both parents at the time of the baby's birth would be even more helpful. Having universal health care coverage in place is also very helpful. And there are more ways that are helpful. Please read Mr. Corey's article to benefit from the entirety of his very thoughtful presentation on this topic!

LGBTQ rights

Obviously, these letters, and the people that they represent, have been in the news for many years. Anti-discrimination laws in place for LGBTQ people are being overturned. In 2016, leaders in North Carolina, a state whose people and terrain I am very fond of, passed and signed legislation into law that is humiliating to LGBTQ people. This legislation concerns protecting others from

---

[*] http://elitedaily.com/news/politics/lower-abortion-clinics/1290840/

LGBTQ people in restrooms. The fact that there are far greater safety issues that aren't being addressed makes me question the motives of the state's legislators and governor. Could "safety" have been a convenient disguise for their real motive? Maybe not, but to this amateur observer of politics and government, it appears that way.[3]

Some feel that LGBTQ designates sinfulness. Others don't. Based on that divide, I will address how I think that people on each side of this divide should treat LGBTQ people. Those who don't equate the LGBTQ designation with sinfulness should love and embrace LGBTQ people and make sure that they are protected from discrimination. Those who do think that the LGBTQ designation can be equated with sinfulness should love and embrace LGBTQ people and make sure that they are protected from discrimination. There should be no difference in their approaches! This should be how we try to approach everyone. Those who feel both that LGBTQ equates with sin and that they should do something about these (LGBTQ) people, other than treating them with complete kindness, would do well to consider the words of Jesus, found in John 8:7: "Let he that is without sin cast the first stone." The judgmental, holier-than-thou attitudes directed toward LGBTQ people certainly explain a lot of the need for anti-discrimination laws for their protection in the first place!

On June 16, 2016, my wife and I attended a very moving and inspirational Service of Lament, mourning the tragic loss of life that took place at the Pulse nightclub in Orlando a few days earlier. Printed on the service program was Matthew 5:4: "Blessed are those who mourn, for they will be comforted." Not enough of us realize the comforting power of God that is available to us if we simply take our burdens to Him. He is always more than willing and ready

---

[3] Update: The law I referred to was partially repealed on March 30, 2017.

to lighten our load if we only reach out to Him for help.

Global warming

There is good evidence for this phenomenon, unless one prefers to get science information from non-mainstream sources, such as political parties and some of the carbon-based energy companies. This is not a political issue, or, at least, it should not be. This is an issue of survival for millions and millions, and possibly billions, of people, not to mention countless other species that God created. I think that we are using and abusing our planet at a rate that exceeds its self-restoration mechanisms!! Do we really want to risk the health of the earth for future generations, and even for our own generation? Opponents of efforts to reduce use of carbon-based energy sources say that these efforts would be too expensive, and would harm the economy. I suspect that if they get their way, any temporary benefit to the economy would soon go away as we struggle to pay for disaster after disaster. Do you think that their descendants would be thankful for their efforts to protect the economy instead of the earth?

The national debt

I thought that our leaders were on the right track in 2010 with the formation of the National Commission on Fiscal Responsibility and Reform (Simpson-Bowles). I may be wrong about this, but this effort appeared to be thwarted by what I think of as the self-planned and self-enacted self-paralysis of Congress. This idea (Simpson-Bowles) should be resurrected and brought to fruition. Furthermore, I would advocate for Warren Buffett's idea that no sitting member of Congress should be eligible for re-election if the budget isn't balanced!

Plenty of economists see economic benefits from maintaining a national debt. But our debt is probably getting close to the point at which it likely would be more detrimental than beneficial, if it is not already at that point. Therefore, I think that we should all start urging our congressional underachievers, I mean Senators and Representatives, to start working again on Simpson-Bowles, or something very similar to it. Since our federal government is possibly going to be spending more on disaster relief in the future, it makes sense to me that we should reduce our national debt while we can, even if tax increases are needed to do so.

Health care

It seems that a high percentage of people who are opposed to Obamacare have never had to worry about getting or paying for health insurance. Ultimately, I think we will go to a system of single payer universal coverage. Does anyone really think that companies are thrilled by the obligation of having to provide health insurance coverage for their employees? And does anyone think that hospitals and physician offices, not to mention the patients themselves, enjoy navigating the medical care payment infrastructure that we currently have, with all of its inefficiencies?

A House Divided

This refers to a worrisome trend in our country. We are becoming more and more divided politically. People are tending to align more and more with party extremes, or something worse. In 1858, Abraham Lincoln, while discussing slave states and free states, said, "A house divided against itself cannot stand." I suspect that he was quoting Jesus (see Mark 3:24 and 25; to get the full context, also read the few verses before those). So, what needs to be done? We need to quit thinking that one side or the other in the political spectrum has a monopoly on right answers and good ideas. We need to quit worshipping at the altar of extremism. We need to tone down our passion for one side or the other. We need to vote for congressional candidates who promise to work with the other side. And we have to realize that it is WE!! who are to blame for our highly dysfunctional Congress! After all, we elected them!

A Prayer for Our Voters to Pray

Lord, thank You for this responsibility and opportunity with which I have been blessed. If You agree that it is important, please inspire my voting. Please help me to make good choices as I vote. And please help me to remember to frequently pray for our elected officials. Please help me to make it a habit to pray that they be blessed with wisdom, compassion, cooperation, courage, perseverance, and peace-seeking. In Jesus' Name, Amen.

A Prayer for Our Lawmakers to Pray

Lord, thank You for both the opportunity and the responsibility with which You have blessed me. Please help me with each and every task at hand. Please help me to remember that I and my party don't necessarily have all of the right answers. Help me to remember that the process of lawmaking works better if we don't work with inflamed passions. In this regard, please help me to remember the practical wisdom attributed to Otto von Bismarck regarding lawmaking ("Laws are like sausages, it is better not to see them being made"). And please help me to remember the inspiring words of a famous Nebraskan, Larry the Cable Guy, whose words are, "Git-R-Done!" If you help me with these issues, Lord, I think that we will be able to accomplish more, and do it more happily! In Jesus' Name, Amen.

A Prayer for Our President to Pray

Lord, thank You for both the responsibility and the opportunity with which You have blessed me. Please be with me and guide me today and every day as I try to do what is right for our country and for the world. Please help me to embrace my opportunities to work with Congress and to try to harvest the best possible results from these opportunities. Please help me to be a positive influence and inspiration for others, both here and abroad. In Jesus' Name, Amen.

A Prayer for Our Supreme Court Justices to Pray

Lord, thank You for both the responsibility and the opportunity with which You have blessed me. Please bless me with the needed wisdom, strength, and courage to follow the letter of the law and not be influenced by politics as I make my judgments. In Jesus' Name, Amen.
Of course, any of the above prayers can be altered a little, as needed, by non-Christians, but I invite them (you) to consider saying or thinking the prayers as written.

My Wish List (for our Congress and President):

1. Adequate funding for scientific research. This should be applied to all branches of science that are felt to be important to our nation and the world. The need for scientific research is great, and is unfortunately

underestimated by many members of our Congress and Administration.
2. Greatly increased efforts by our government to reduce our over-consumption of carbon-based energy sources, and greatly increased efforts to find other ways of ameliorating climate change.
3. Single payer universal health care coverage.
4. Significant reduction of our national debt by implementing some tax increases, improving our system of taxation, and cutting spending in areas that seem wasteful or not vital.
5. A thorough and very humane approach to immigration and the many issues surrounding it.
6. Removal of assault weapons from the general population, allowing America to become the safe place that most of us desire.
7. Continued efforts to overcome discrimination directed at any group.
8. Better preparation for disasters, including having adequate capital reserves to fund disaster relief. Along with this there should be strong coordination between the government agencies that address disaster relief and charitable organizations that do the same.
9. Employment of more Americans to fix our aging transportation infrastructure (roads and bridges), to build more mass transit systems, and to help improve our system of transmitting electricity, and
10. Equalization of per-student financial support for all public-school districts in the country.

Render unto Caesar

What I am now addressing is the danger of mixing faith and politics. As I said earlier, we strive to have separation of church and state, but it is difficult for us to separate politics from our faith within the confines of our minds. While I suspect that this has been done, probably many times by many authors, I nevertheless want to somewhat concisely present some of my thoughts on the dangers of mixing our faith and politics.

I think that we can safely allow ourselves, on an individual basis, to let our faith and our politics mix. Doing this may help us decide how to vote, for whom and for what. I think that another way of saying this is summed up nicely by the expression "vote your conscience."

But it shouldn't go further than that.

If we allow too much of the blending of our faith and our politics to extend beyond the confines of our own minds, we quickly enter the realm of trying to push our ideas derived from this blending onto others. This area is dangerous because both faith and politics have such profound influences on the strength of our convictions, and when blended together, the influences of faith and politics are even stronger. And our convictions aren't always right. And when our convictions are very wrong, there is especially great danger. There is a built-in safeguard when everyone votes according to his or her own conscience. If everyone is voting his or her conscience, then there is not the danger of large numbers of people being misled by someone in a leadership position who has allowed his or her own mistakes in judgement to extend to others. When we try to promote our faith based ideas on how to vote to others, we run the risk of depriving some people of their ability to vote their own conscience. This was an extremely important consideration in 2016.

I think many people see no problem with allowing their faith and politics to blend, and then using the ideas derived from this mix to influence others. I think that their idea can be stated roughly as follows: "If my faith and politics are good for me, they are good for everyone else. And I think that this is how God wants me to act!" It seems to me that this phenomenon has become more common in the last thirty to forty years, but maybe it has always been common and I have just become more aware of it. Many evangelical leaders in particular appear to be guiding their followers not only in matters of faith, but also in political matters. Specifically, they are telling their followers how to vote. I used to not pay much attention to their endorsements, but recently I have, and in 2016 I was disturbed by the endorsements of many of them.

Regarding the thought that God is in favor of us actively pushing an agenda derived from blending our faith and politics, I say, "No!!!! This violates the system of free will that God gave us!" I think that our world operates according to free will to embrace either good or evil. I think that God knew that this was the best system for His children (us) to live under while living in a world in which there would be continuous exposure to a balance of good and evil. I think that the system of free will helps us develop and hone our faith, and God is more than available to assist us with this process when we ask Him.

Pushing our blended faith and political agendas is also contrary to the spirit of our Constitution, even if it not necessarily against the law. But when pushed too far, it probably also reaches the point of breaking the law. When we are too successful in pushing such agendas, it almost certainly makes people of other faiths feel rather uneasy about our country and its government. Depending on our agendas, those in minorities of other designations (racial, ethnic, LGBTQ, etc.) also likely feel the same sense of unease.

Probably countless well-meaning Christians embrace the blending of politics and faith because they think that it will bring more people to their (our) faith, but I think that it is counterproductive. I think that it actually drives just as many people away from our faith as it brings to our faith – possibly even more. When we employ an aggressive manner to promote our faith, what we are ultimately doing is inflicting our faith on others. It isn't well received. This tactic gives Christianity a bad name, and it also gives Jesus a bad name. I also address some related ideas in "Our interactions with people of other faiths."

I think that there is only one good way for us to blend our faith and politics as we work in government or politics. This can be called "living our faith." When using this approach, we try to do what is right for people, with our primary focus being on them, rather than on us or our own agendas. With this approach, one can even incorporate the idea of "what would Jesus do?" within one's own mind. One then lets his or her good actions be shining, inspiring examples to others, without being pushy with faith-related words or preaching. If others ask about our motivations for doing what seems right and good, we should be prepared to give a limited, but cautious answer, such as, "Some of my ideas are based on my faith, and my faith is this or that, but while I am acting in a political or official governmental capacity, I don't feel that it is appropriate for me to expound further on my faith." When one's job in politics or government is over, then I don't think that one has to restrain one's explanations as much, but we should remember that the opinions of a former elected official or politician, even then, can continue to have a political impact. The safest approach is to follow these rules: Those who want to preach should not enter politics, and those who want to be politicians should not preach. The exception would be that if one lives in a country with a state-sponsored religion, but this does not include the United States. Considering the Constitution that we have, we should fully respect the spirit of freedom of religion.

Unfortunately, many of us think that freedom of religion is great, as long as its benefits only apply to adherents of our own religion. Christians should remember that Jesus said, "Render unto Caesar what is Caesar's, and unto God what is God's." If we allow our faith and politics to mix while we are in a political or governmental role, we get Jesus' command mixed-up; we render unto Caesar what is God's, and vice versa.

Earlier I wrote that I was disturbed by the endorsements of many of the evangelical leaders in 2016. Let me explain by citing several verses from the New Testament. The verses are Second Timothy 3:1–5, which read, "This know also, that in the last days perilous times shall come. For men shall be lovers of their own selves, covetous, boasters, proud, blasphemers, disobedient to parents, unthankful, unholy, Without natural affection, trucebreakers, false accusers, incontinent, fierce, despisers of those that are good, Traitors, heady, highminded, lovers of pleasures more than lovers of God; Having a form of godliness, but denying the power thereof: from such turn away."

And because I am so concerned, I will restate these words from another version of the Bible to make sure that the message is clear! Here are the same verses from the New Century Version, "Remember this! In the last days there will be many troubles, because people will love themselves, love money, brag, and be proud. They will say evil things against others and will not obey their parents or be thankful or be the kind of people God wants. They will not love others, will refuse to forgive, will gossip, and will not control themselves. They will be cruel, will hate what is good, will turn against their friends, and will do foolish things without thinking. They will be conceited, will love pleasure instead of God, and will act as if they serve God but will not have his power. Stay away from those people."

Now I continue with the explanation. These verses are essentially a list of behaviors that are obviously pleasing to Satan but not to God. All of us at least occasionally behave in a manner pleasing to Satan, but if we are fairly successfully attempting to live righteous lives that are in accordance with how God wants us to live, the words, "Stay away from those people" don't apply to us. But if we consistently and frequently exhibit many of the behaviors on the list, then those last five words do apply to us, from the perspective of others.

A related point that I want to make is that freedom of religion also includes freedom to ignore your religion. If your conscience says that it is acceptable to go against the words of Second Timothy 3:1–5, you obviously can do so. And, of course, the free will system that God the Father gave us allows you to do so.

And one more slightly related point is that no major political party has a monopoly on Christianity! The members of one party seem to be more vocal about their connection with Christianity, however.

Satan absolutely loves it when we go too far with our blending of faith and politics; this is one of his favorite playgrounds. He further blesses this union (of faith and politics) with the gift of self-righteousness. With this blessing he is able to remove the love of God from our faith-based ideas. As a result, he is able to hijack our good intentions and transform them into his intentions. Our actions then become pleasing to him.

Conversely, I think that God looks disapprovingly on blending faith and politics because it tells Him that we have stronger faith in our political system than we have in prayer as a means of transforming our faith-based ideas into reality!

Afterthoughts, Thanksgiving week, 2016

Number one on my list of things for which I am thankful is God's love, which surpasses all human understanding! God has blessed me in so many ways!

One of the many blessings that God has given me is another answered prayer. A couple of months ago I started asking God for help with my own self-righteousness. Recently, as a result of this prayer being answered, I have realized that what you have just read in "Render unto Caesar....." contains some of my own self-righteousness. I now more fully realize that my criticism of blending faith and politics was directed at those who are called conservatives. I must add that those who are called liberals also suffer from the affliction of self-righteousness in their interactions with conservatives.

No matter whose faith-based ideas are being pushed in the political arena, Satan is able to remove the element of God's love from these ideas with his gift of self-righteousness. This may have something to do with liberal ideas, such as public assistance programs, not being as successful as they were hoped to be. God's love is better shared on an individual basis, such as between family members or between friends. Charities also are better suited to preserve the element of God's love than government programs. But we still need the safety net provided by government programs.

It seems that those on either side of the political spectrum can easily see the flaws of the ideas of those on the opposite side, but have trouble seeing the flaws of their own ideas.

I also recognize that use of the verses from Second Timothy represents a degree of self-righteousness on my part, but I also feel the verses were used to make a point that needed to be made!

And I am thankful for a dear friend whose faith is greater than mine and whose words helped me to get my priorities straight a few days after the election. We had greeted each other, and in response to him mentioning the news of the week, I told him that I was depressed. He told me, "I'm not." I then asked him if he was a supporter of the winner. Within two seconds I knew, without doubt, that he was not. And his following words I will always remember. "We reap what we sow!"

After our meeting I thought about some of the things about which I have written. One was that the election is a "thing of this world", and its ultimate importance to us is limited to our earthly lives. If we are "all in" regarding our faith in Jesus, we have absolutely no reason to be depressed about the results of the election or the realization that we are living in a divided nation. We are to be positive because our faith helps us to see beyond our earthly concerns. But we are not to turn our backs on the world. There has never been a greater need for us to live our faith. As we joyfully go about our "work" of living our faith, we can be further energized with these words from Philippians 4:13, "I can do all things through Christ who strengthens me." (NKJV)

And regarding the statement, "We reap what we sow", this is consistent with God's will being done. He gave us free will, and we used this gift of free will to sow our seeds. The seeds have sprouted and the plants have emerged from the soil. But what exactly is it that we will reap? Finding out will be "interesting", to say the least! Let us not be dismayed or overwhelmed by our harvest! Keep the faith!

Living Our Faith

Ancient wisdom

I think that it was our younger son who once asked me why I liked to watch so many programs on ancient history. My first thought was, "What is there that could possibly be any better to watch?", but I didn't answer in that way. I think that I answered something like, "I think that there is a lot of ancient wisdom that has been lost. I think that it might be helpful for us if we could recover some of it." I was thinking in terms of all the collected writings that had been destroyed by fire in the Great Library of Alexandria, and many other similar, but smaller, losses elsewhere. I continue to enjoy watching programs on ancient history (my nerd shows, as I call them), as well as reading about ancient history.

I think that my answer was partly right. There is a lot of ancient wisdom that would be very helpful to us, but it has been lost only by disuse and disinterest, not by fire, etc. Fortunately, it isn't hard to find. This wisdom, in written form, can be found in homes throughout the world. Even if it isn't available in book form, it is available on the internet. Of course, in certain parts of the world it is both difficult and dangerous to try to access this wisdom.

The Bible is the collection of ancient wisdom that I am referring to. And ancient is probably not the best term for describing it, because it is also modern wisdom. Even though our accoutrements have changed, we are still basically the same as the people of the past. We are still equipped with the same human nature. We still have the same free will to be influenced by the forces of good and evil. We still have the same (and only) God. And we still have the same (and only) tempter (Satan). The wisdom saturating the Bible is equally useful today as it was 2000 years ago (in fact, it may be more useful today than at any previous time; see "Enough, already!").

The people who say that the Bible is outdated and outmoded are the ones who are not willing to give it a complete chance. I admit that the Bible can be hard to read and to understand. Understanding often requires some mentoring from a more experienced reader of the Bible; I often need the insight of others to help me to understand parts of the Bible.

Repetition helps. I have read the New Testament about six times and the Old Testament one and one half times (I'm halfway through my second reading of the Old Testament) and while I don't consider myself anywhere close to an expert on the Bible, it is very satisfying to gain new insight about Biblical wisdom. Just like Coach Collier [I mention him in another story], I often think, "Why didn't I see that before?" And sometimes the acquisition of new knowledge and insight from the Bible is much more than satisfying; it can be powerful; it may lead to trembling, moist eyes, etc.

Ancient Wisdom, Part Two (Additional Thoughts on the Bible)

Some people dismiss the Bible because they say that it can't be proven. Personally, after experiencing my unusual events, I have no need for the Bible to be proven. Others, however, do have this need, or want.

One of my favorite stories in the Bible is that of the Children of Israel leaving Egypt in a mass exodus, of course with the help and guidance of God. Many people say that there is no proof for the people of Israel ever being in Egypt or for them making a mass exodus. And they are right, at least according to most historians and archaeologists. Regarding the lack of proof for the people of Israel existing in Egypt for approximately four hundred years, I have this thought. If you were the ruler of Egypt right after the Exodus, would you want to leave any evidence of the nation of slaves that had just humiliated you? Absolutely not! I suspect that there was a widespread and systematic effort to erase any evidence that the Children of Israel ever existed in Egypt, and I suspect that such an effort would have had the cooperation of most Egyptians. And there wouldn't be any record of this effort because such a record of it would defeat the purpose of the effort. Of course, this is just my own speculation, and I can't prove any of it. And if you don't think that such an effort was or is possible, consider the Holocaust deniers of our times. While this obviously isn't a perfect comparison, I do think that it demonstrates the lengths that people will go to erase historical memory.

My other thought regards proof of the Exodus. Again, most historians and archaeologists say that there isn't proof of this. I don't blame them. There probably isn't sufficient proof to meet their professional standards. Personally, I have no doubt that the Exodus occurred. And, of course, my statement offers and provides no proof. That said, there is some very fascinating reading available on this topic if you do an internet search for Red Sea crossing on the Gulf of Aqaba.

There's power in them thar words!

This scenario borrows from the Gold Rush days of Georgia and California, and also from Mark Twain. Imagine a group of three or four miners sitting around a campfire. Sitting with them and trying to tend to their spiritual needs is an itinerant preacher (one who might have gotten his call "direct"). He asks one of the miners, "Jeb, why did you come all the way to California?", all the while knowing how Jeb would answer. Jeb replied, "Well, Mr. Preacher, I hear tell, there's gold in them thar hills!" Mr. Preacher then answered back, while pointing to his Bible, "Well Jeb, there's power in them thar words! As a matter of fact, there's way more power in them thar words than the power of all of the gold in them thar hills!"

The fact that words have power has always been known. The writers of the Bible knew it. The Gospel of John begins with the words, "In the beginning was the Word, and the Word was with God, and the Word was God." To me, these are very powerful words!

In case you have doubts about the power of words, I will tell you a story from my days in the ER.....One of the doctors who worked in our ER had just arrived for the 1 AM to 7 AM shift. He had just picked up a chart to read when a nurse got his attention. He always liked working with this nurse. She was smart, efficient, witty, and cheerful. She told him about a child who sounded somewhat more ill than usual. She asked him if he wanted her to get lab tests started while he was seeing his first patient. He had felt stressed and cranky upon arrival at the ER, and he had already decided that he wasn't going to be slowed down by anything possibly unnecessary. Without giving credit to the nurse's concern and without much thought, he immediately answered, "I don't want any freakin' tests!" Immediately, he sensed his blunder when he saw the letdown on her face. And when he saw the patient that she told him about, tests were ordered.... Their friendship was never the same from that point on. She left the ER within a few months. He never did learn where she went from the ER...Incidentally, and fortunately for him, he was able to retire a few years after the events of this story took place. He moved to a warmer climate, a place where he has plenty of time and opportunity to combine two of his favorite activities, bicycling and pondering the power of words, which includes frequently pondering the incredible power of incredible words!

Fast forward to the political "spectacle" we have been witnessing since the summer of 2015 (the word "abomination" also comes to mind). Many hurtful words have been said, and many more will be said – "before all is said and done." Do you suppose that those speaking these hurtful words will ever feel any remorse?

Let's now look to the positive. Positive words also can have immense power. For example, all of the various ways of saying and meaning, "I love you." Along those lines, words of forgiveness also have immense power!

Now let's look at the Bible. The Bible contains the most powerful words in human history! It is full of powerful words, but for me, two sets of verses come to mind. I will start with John 6:68 and 69, but first, I have to set the scene with verses 66 and 67: "From that time many of His disciples went back, and walked no more with Him. Then said Jesus unto the twelve, 'Will ye also go away?'" Verse 68 then reads, "Then Simon Peter answered Him, 'Lord, to whom shall we go? Thou hast the words of eternal life.'" Verse 69 continues this thought with some additional powerful words, "And we believe and are sure that Thou art that Christ, the Son of the living God." The other verse that comes to mind contains the words of Christ, as they appear in John 3:16, "For God so loved the world, that He gave His only begotten Son, that whosoever believeth in Him should not perish, but have everlasting life." Truly powerful words, indeed, and powerful enough to provide us with a summary of the New Testament in one verse. I recommend reading the verses surrounding this most famous verse; there you will find additional statements on salvation and lack thereof.

Everyone should find their own words of power in the Bible. You can turn to these words for hope, encouragement, and peace in times of despair, trouble, fear, sadness, sorrow, feeling unworthy, and so on. I suspect that many people use Psalm 23 for some of these purposes. And you may want to find some celebratory words for good times. Oh, Yahoo!

Always remember the power of words!

Could I be part of the problem?

During the summer of 2016, two things, frequently reported in the news and very much related to each other in my opinion, inspired me to write this chapter. One is the increasing impact of terrorism, both domestically and internationally. The other is a new feature of our ongoing plague of mass casualty shootings; now our police forces are being targeted by angry individuals with guns. It is understandable that those who committed these horrific actions would have some anger, but their actions are in no way justifiable!

Why are we so afflicted by ever-increasing violence? My answers will likely be overly simplistic and perhaps too short, and only be partial answers at that, but they are worth considering nevertheless.

We humans have always had an inability to live in harmony, at least for more than short periods of time. I blame this problem on Satan. Those of you who don't believe in Satan can simply substitute human nature for Satan. I don't think that we are necessarily worse people than the people of times past. I think that if we could transplant people from the past into our modern world, they would quickly acquire our current behavioral characteristics. Why our problem with violence seems to be worse now is due to a variety of factors, I think, and I realize that I will undoubtedly be omitting some of the contributing factors here.

Increasing population density is likely a contributing factor. More and more people are competing for ever-smaller pieces of the pie, so to speak. But I think that even more important yet are our uses and misuses of modern technology. With modern technology, we have available to us all sorts of information, and we have it available almost instantly. There are many very positive benefits of our modern technology, but there are also many negatives. Many of us tend to immerse ourselves in information that is to our liking. This may seem innocent enough at first, but if we aren't careful, we will soon regard people with opposing viewpoints as idiots, or, worse yet, as evil. And the almost instant nature of our modern communications and information access takes away the benefit of the long, slow fuse that was part of information acquisition and sharing in the past. When we have built up enough of a powder keg of negative feelings toward other people and ideas, any new information that we receive and that we perceive as negative may serve to quickly spark an explosion of the powder keg. In the past, when we had less ability to immerse ourselves in only one viewpoint, our powder kegs were smaller, and the slowness of communications gave more time for better judgement to prevail before the spark in the fuse could reach the powder keg. We therefore had the ability to extinguish the spark before the explosion, so to speak.

Our current ease of acquiring arsenals of deadly weapons is another factor that aids in the effectiveness and impact of our inhumanity toward others.

So, what are we to do about this? One suggestion that we frequently hear from politicians is to place a new emphasis on law and order. Upon hearing new calls for such an emphasis during the recent political campaign, that sounded good for a second or two, but then I quickly realized that it likely wouldn't help. Please don't misunderstand me. I like the idea of everyone being law-abiding. But increased emphasis on law and order won't do anything to ease the anger and despair that many people feel and that lead some to react with violence. And too much emphasis on law and order might result in our government resembling the repressive police states, such as Nazi Germany.

Then what can be done, if increased emphasis on law and order won't help? My answer will likely seem stupid, pointless, and a waste of time to many, but I truly think that there is only one thing that will help us recover from our affliction of violence. And that one thing is God's love!

If you believe in God, you might reasonably ask, "Doesn't He already love us? And it doesn't appear to me that His love is doing anything to relieve us of our problem with hate and violence." Then I would answer, "True enough. But it is still the answer. We simply need much, much more of His love." You might then ask, "Then why doesn't God just give us much, much more of His love, since He can surely see that we are in need of it?" I would then answer, "God doesn't do this because we haven't asked Him, or haven't asked Him in a sufficient manner."... Remember that I think we live with free will in a world filled with equal opportunities for us to seek both good and evil. I believe that God wants to bless us with an overabundance of His love, but first we need to sufficiently ask Him for this blessing. We can't pray meekly or without full faith and expect results. We need to empower our prayers with boldness, confidence, and all the power of our non-sinful emotions. Don't try to empower your prayers with hate, for example. Emotional energy derived from feelings of hurt, pain, suffering, anguish, misery, depression, love, compassion, and empathy (and there are probably more) can be very effective in energizing and empowering our prayers. I believe that prayer power is additive or cumulative. The more like-minded people that we have praying with one accord, or the higher the energy of an individual's prayer, the greater the blessing from God will be. To borrow a favorite word that my pastor uses in this regard, God wants to be able to 'unleash' His power to help us, but it is We! who need to sufficiently engage Him and ask Him! Because of His respect for and adherence to the system of free will that he gave us, He needs us to be the initiators and enablers so that He can act. I am certain that there are occasional exceptions to this system when He has another purpose in mind, but I think that this is the way it (His system of answering prayers) usually works.

I will add a common example from our sports world to help give you a feeling for prayer power, even though the example itself isn't necessarily connected with prayer. After hard fought contests, often what is said about the winner is, "He (or she, or they) wanted it more!"...... When we pray, we need to "want it more!" And, unlike the sports world, with prayer there doesn't have to be a loser; God has more than enough love and blessings for everyone, if only we would ask Him sufficiently!

To those of us who don't believe in God and who thought that I would write something different, I ask, "What did you expect that I would write? Look again at the title of the book, for heaven's sake!"

Now, in case you are wondering if I will ever get to the question that I posed at the beginning of this piece, I just have (gotten to it). Before I started writing this chapter, I asked myself that question, and I'm not proud to say that, yes, I am part of the problem leading to our increasing violence. Despite my most deadly weapon being my car, and despite having strong faith in Jesus, God the Father, and the Holy Spirit (our Holy Trinity), and despite praying a lot, I still am part of the problem. Some of you might be asking, "How is that possible?", and others of you, especially those who disagree with what I have written, might be thinking, "Of course you are part of the problem!" I am part of the problem because of all my missed opportunities to spread the love of God. It is impossible for me to list all of these missed opportunities, but I will try to list some of them. When I don't establish eye contact with a person I encounter while walking, and don't greet him or her, I have missed an opportunity. When I don't stop to render aid to someone who appears to be in need, I have missed an opportunity. When I don't at least offer food and water, or a voucher or gift certificate for the same, as well as eye contact and encouraging words to someone whom we often call a "panhandler" and who is asking me for help, I have missed an opportunity. When I don't pray for my "enemies", I have missed an opportunity. When I don't pray for politicians and leaders with whom I disagree, I have missed an opportunity. When I don't pray for the supporters of the leaders and politicians with whom I disagree, I have missed an opportunity. When I don't pray for politicians and leaders with whom I agree, I have missed an opportunity. When I am stingy with donations to my favorite charities, all of whom are very helpful to people in need, I have missed opportunities. When I avoid being friendly to someone of a race or religion different from mine, I have really missed an opportunity! When I don't tell my Representative and my Senators that I want our nation to be able to live up to the words of Emma Lazarus' poem, The New Colossus, which speak of the Statue of Liberty, I have really missed an opportunity! The list could go on and on.......

    I must keep in mind that a person who committed violence may have been just one friendly encounter, one touch of God's love, away from having changed his or her mind about harming others, and it may have been me who missed that opportunity!

    So, what is my plan? I'm going to pray more fervently and more often for God to shower us with His love, and to fill us with His love, so that it overflows from our hearts and touches others as we encounter them. I'm going to pray that I have God's help in spreading His love, so that I don't miss my opportunities, and so that I don't withhold His love from anyone, especially those who look different from me or worship differently from me. I'm going to pray that I receive frequent inspiration to love my "enemies" and those whose political thoughts differ from mine. I'm going to pray that we, including myself, not get too immersed in, or too carried away with the extremes of politics, since it is not only nonproductive, but also maddening, to allow ourselves to become excessively polarized. I'm going to pray that we, including myself, restrain ourselves from letting our faiths and politics mix, and that we remember that this can be a dangerous mix. (The reason I mention this last prayer is the example of Hitler. Although there is evidence that he privately disdained Christianity, he used religion to mobilize the masses and he often said that he was doing God's work. Thankfully, such a thing couldn't happen here in America, or could it?)

    I'm also going to try to change my actions and behaviors so that more of God's love is spread to where it is needed, which is actually everywhere on earth. Obviously, I need your help here, so please help me with this effort. I'm going to try to think more prayers for the people whom I see in my daily life; I'm going to ask God to bless these people in the manner in which He knows they need to be blessed, and to shower them with His love. And I'm going to try to remember to thank God for all of the opportunities that He gives me to share His love…Oh, Yahoo! And Amen!

Reflections on spigotology

I've thought about this topic (spigotology) for a long time, although the name is relatively new to me, coming on March 24, 2016. In case you are wondering if this is connected to March Madness and bracketology, I didn't envision it that way, but there might actually be a weak connection between them. I didn't initially think that it had anything to do with beer, either, but after thinking about it for a while, I can see how Ben Franklin and those who align with his ideas and outlook on life would see a connection.

What this is about is a gift, a gift that I used to think of as an affliction. I have the gift that spigotology addresses. So do lots of other people. The most famous person with this gift that I know of is former House Speaker John Boehner, who might be blessed with an even greater gift of this type than I am. The name of the gift, which also came to me today, is "a well-functioning Spigot Control System (SCS)."

Let me explain a little more about the SCS. It has within it the Spigot Control Center Receiver (SCCR), which is roughly the opposite of a BSO'Meter. Those of you equipped with a well functioning BSO'Meter may now be sensing some activity in your meter, but please bear with me! The SCS contains, of course, the Spigot Control Center (SCC), the SCCR (which you already met), and the spigots. The SCCR provides input to the SCC, which, in turn, controls the spigots. The spigots help regulate flow from lacrimal glands. In much simpler terms, the spigots control tear flow. The SCS helps initiate and regulate a chain of events that leads to tear flow.

After spending years thinking about how my SCS works and what its workings might represent, I have come to a few conclusions. The SCCR is most likely to be activated when it receives signals that something great is in the vicinity. Mine tends to be activated at church, including regular services, funerals, and even weddings. It isn't necessarily connected with sadness, although sad occasions and thoughts will also activate it. More often, I am completely happy when mine is activated.

Last year, during a church service, I had great inspiration from a line in a hymn. The line helped me to understand my SCCR much more clearly. It also told me that the SCCR might have connections with something with which we are more familiar, but understand poorly. The name of this "something" is "soul." The line in the hymn, the name of which I don't remember, is "You overwhelm my soul!" I immediately thought, "That's it! That is what I have been looking for!"

This gets me to my thoughts on the soul. For a long time, I have wondered, what constitutes a soul and where is it located? My best concise answer is that the soul is a small piece of God. I think that God donates a little bit of Himself to be housed in each person. This sounds somewhat like the Holy Spirit that we are blessed to have within us. I don't completely know where the Holy Spirit ends and the soul starts. However, I do think that our soul is "stamped" with our own identity and that the Holy Spirit within us isn't. I think that our soul and our share of, or input from, the Holy Spirit (or Holy Spirit App, as I now like to think of our share of the Holy Spirit) are probably separate, but there are likely communication links between them. As to where the soul is located, I don't know. It seems to me that it should be located in our head, or heart, or somewhere in between. And our Holy Spirit App is probably not far from our soul.

Back to the line in the hymn, "You overwhelm my soul!" I think that somehow our soul, probably with help from the Holy Spirit, sends signals to our SCCR when it senses that we are in the presence of something great, something that reminds our soul of God. For those of us with well-functioning SCSs, we know that we may be in the presence of something great when the tears start appearing. And usually when this happens, I feel happy and a little (or very) overwhelmed.

Now let's return to the question of where the soul is located. It likely shares space with the eyes, since it seems that tears have a cleansing effect on the soul. And maybe the flow of tears represents the "spin cycle" that follows the washing of our soul. (But, of course, the soul doesn't get completely washed by tears. This requires our forgiveness paid for by Jesus and our ultimate removal from the influences of Satan). In my mind, these thoughts are consistent with the old adage that the eyes are the windows to the soul. They are also consistent with the words of Jesus, found in Matthew 6:22: "The light of the body is the eye...."

A final observation from spigotology: if I try to fight it (the flow of tears), it only intensifies. Sometimes I can try to calm down the response by turning to distracting thoughts. But I don't want to completely go to distracting thoughts, because that would also defeat my attempts to find the inspiration that I was seeking. So, in conclusion, after all of my study on this topic, I have learned that it is just best to go with the flow.

Afterthought

Perhaps the SCS is meant to function at a high level in people with depression. Perhaps it points them to Someone who likely would help them to improve their depression, that Someone being God. It may not be a quick fix because strengthening our faith is usually slow and somewhat difficult for us. Of course, I will offer my usual advice, "It won't hurt, and it might help!" (After thinking again about this, it occurred to me that Mr. Boehner and I, as well as many others, may have a normal situation for men, a situation that remains unspoiled by teaching about manliness. I realized today that I don't ever remember being taught at home that tears are bad, and that crying needs to be suppressed. Any teaching in this regard came from outside of my family. And I recall seeing my dad with moist eyes a few times at church, and a few times at home. So, now, I'm even more OK with my "gift").

Proud of our faith?

A few months ago, while biking through our downtown area, I saw a bumper sticker that got my attention, as bumper stickers often do. It read, "This is a Christian Nation." This didn't sound quite right to me. Don't get me wrong. I don't have a problem with our nation being a Christian nation, if, in fact, it is one. But I also don't have a problem with our nation's constitutional promise of freedom of religion, with people living up to that promise, and with welcoming people of any faith. In fact, I would very much like all of us, including me, to be welcoming to people of any and all faiths.

I have at least two problems with the statement, "This is a Christian Nation." One is that this seems too much like "in your face" Christianity, or the "it's my way or the highway" version of Christianity. To me, this is the version of Christianity that led to the Crusades (which did very little, if any, good, and a whole lot of harm). This smacks of the type of Christianity practiced by those who seek to impose their faith and faith-related ideas for government on others (I have no doubt that most of them are very sincere and believe that they are doing the right thing; I simply disagree with their approach and attitude). "This is a Christian Nation" is not the statement of a "What would Jesus do?" Christian. There is no humility in the statement. If you read the first nine verses of the Beatitudes (Matthew 5:3–11), you can see that there is no statement saying, "Blessed are the proud." It's the poor in spirit, those who mourn, the meek, those who hunger and thirst after righteousness, the merciful, the pure in heart, the peacemakers, those who are persecuted for righteousness' sake, and those who are reviled and persecuted for Jesus' sake who are blessed!

There is a place for pride in our faith, but our pride should be in God (Father, Son, and Holy Spirit) and in what He has done for us. There is no place for us being proud that we are Christians. Conversely, there is no place for us to be ashamed that we are Christians. We should feel thankfulness and gratitude for our faith, which is the path to salvation. We do not choose our faith (some of us may think we did). Our faith is given to us as a gift from God, who moved through our parents or others to kindle the faith within us. We are not to look down on people of other faiths, or those without faith. If we were in their situations, with their circumstances, then their faith (or lack thereof) would probably be our faith (or lack thereof). We must be open to witnessing for our faith, but if we try to inflict our faith on others, they will more likely be driven away from our faith than brought closer to it.

The second problem that I have with the bumper sticker message is that although we are supposedly a Christian nation, this isn't something our observations can readily tell us. At least, not if we are thinking in terms of "What would Jesus do?", which is the ideal for which we should strive. What we might find, however, is plenty of Christians with a faith of convenience and plenty with a crusader's mindset.

So, I would rather see a bumper sticker that asks, "What would Jesus do?" If you are at all aware of the many recent troubling events in our nation and the rest of the world, it is my hope that you would agree with me on this point.

Long-term investing

Before I get to long-term investing, I want to share some of my thoughts on short-term investing. I think that we should concentrate on short-term investing for our big needs in life (paying for our home, paying for education, and saving for retirement). Isn't that what you have been hearing from others as well? If you plan wisely, diversify your investments, spend moderately, at most, and are patient, short-term investing should meet your financial needs.

In case you are questioning this notion, I should probably tell you that what I mean by short-term investing is a little different from what is commonly meant. I see short-term investing as involving investments that are held for at least two years, but preferably five or more years. "Wait a minute!", you are probably thinking. "That sounds like long-term investing to me!"

Let me clarify. I think that long-term investing is how we save for our really important goal(s). Short-term investing, in which investments are mostly held five years or more, is how we save for the goals that aren't quite as important as our long-term goals. These are the goals that I mentioned earlier, the ones that may be 10–30 years away.

There is a term that can be applied to investments held less than two years (and I realize that financial advisors usually call these investments short-term investments). This term is spelled G-A-M-B-L-I-N-G. I'm not inexperienced with gambling. Even now I have minor investments in the lottery. There is a problem with this type of investing, however. If we get too caught up in it, money becomes our addiction, or our "idol". Our worship of this "idol" is called greed. Greed is especially dangerous for our long-term investments and associated goal(s). Therefore, if we participate in this type of investing, we should keep it at a safe level, a "hobby" level. This type of investing remains safer yet for us if we share some of the proceeds from these investments in a manner approved by the original Author of long-term investing. The safest of all options for this type of investment is avoidance.

This gets me to long-term investing, and the goal(s) that our long-term investments help achieve. Jesus spoke of this type of investing in Matthew 6:19–21, "Lay not up for yourselves treasures upon earth, where moth and rust doth corrupt, and where thieves break through and steal: But lay up for yourselves treasures in heaven, where neither moth nor rust doth corrupt, and where thieves do not break through and steal: For where your treasure is, there will your heart be also." As I typed this, I was in awe of the wisdom and love that God (Jesus in this case) gives us. I felt trembling and my eyes moistened!

So don't attach too much importance to money. Money is important to help meet our earthly needs, those same needs of our descendants, if we are fortunate enough to have descendants and to be able to leave something for them, and the needs of others whom we want to help (this includes helping spread the good news about Jesus to others), but it has no safe and healthy importance beyond that. And I'm sure that you have all heard the saying, "You can't take it with you."

Limited by our success

This part is dedicated to those who don't believe that the experiences I wrote about in 'Unusual occurrences' are true. And this is not, by any means, an attempt to speak down to or otherwise retaliate. There probably were periods in my life when I would have had trouble believing the stories of these occurrences.

My point in writing this part is to say that it is too bad that more of us can't believe this type of story. I think that all of us, or, at least most of us, like to believe that there is something greater than ourselves. For many of us, the greatest things that we know about are the modern day technological wonders. And as great as our modern toys and gadgets are, they have their limits. Their greatness is constrained by the limits of human ingenuity.

I suspect that some part of our brain functions in a way that helps us to be impressed with great things; for this story, I will call this area our Great Things Recognition Center (GTRC). This is similar to what I wrote about in Reflections on spigotology; the same area of our brain may even be involved with both stories, in which case, two different names aren't really necessary.

In modern times, we have had many toys and gadgets that our GTRCs help us recognize as impressive. I think that with all of our impressive developments, our GTRCs become somewhat numbed, and don't respond as they should. Sometimes we don't have much power, sensitivity, and range remaining in our GTRCs to adequately register when something impressive comes along. Even if they do, they get used to functioning only at a level suited for manmade things (their ranges become constrained, or limited). And we get used to the idea that there is nothing greater to get excited about. And when something even greater (something from the supernatural realm, something from God!) makes an appearance, our GTRCs don't know how to respond, and we simply say, "I don't believe that!"

I think that the people living 1,000 years ago would have had a much easier time believing the stories of my unusual occurrences. Their GTRCs wouldn't have been worn out from being used too frequently; in fact, they would have been capable of operating at their full, normal ranges of capability and recognizing the greatness level of something from God.

The arguments against the claim are many. Surely people living 1,000 years ago weren't as smart as we are today. Surely people back then were more naive, more superstitious and completely lacked the sophisticated knowledge we enjoy today. They couldn't possibly have recognized great things when they saw them.

Or could they?

First, regarding their smartness and capabilities, who do you think would fare better if placed on a desert island without the benefit of any of mankind's inventions, we or they?......And while people living 1,000 years ago might not have had the scientific and technical knowledge we do today, the upper limit of their knowledge, on average, was probably greater than that of modern people because the upper limit of their knowledge, on average, was much closer to God than ours is. The average upper limit of our knowledge today is definitely far below the level of God, since most of us probably don't spend too much time thinking about God. We are too busy being immersed in our 'things of this world', which surely are much 'greater' than the things of this world 1,000 years ago. In other words, we have become limited by our success!

Living one's faith as a medical professional

Countless people live their faith at work, not only in the medical field, but in all walks of life. I am sure that many are able do this without having to think about it, while others must make more of a conscious effort to do so. In the early 1990s, I started making more of a conscious effort to live my faith at work after our pastor preached on this topic. Prior to that time, I had no routine or well organized thoughts regarding this objective. From the early 1990s until I retired at the end of 2014, my efforts to live my faith at work were a work in progress. I frequently failed to live up to this ideal. I think that my efforts improved as time went on, but I never perfected them (it likely had something to do with being human).

Obviously (I hope), I am writing from the perspective of a Christian. To people of other faiths, you can modify my approach to fit your faith, but I invite and encourage you to try my approach without modification. And, of course, some of what I write on this topic doesn't necessarily require one to have faith at all. And, as you are undoubtedly aware, much of this information can be easily applied to any job or profession.

First and foremost, be familiar with the concept of "What would Jesus do?" To be familiar with this concept, it is necessary to be familiar with the New Testament, especially the gospels (the first four books of the New Testament). Perhaps the quickest way to get started learning "What would Jesus do?" is to read chapters five, six, and seven of Matthew.

As you learn more and more about living your faith, you can start practicing what you have learned. One action that helped me focus on living my faith at work was to think a very short prayer as I was preparing to see a patient. The prayer can be as simple as "Dear Lord, please help me to be as helpful as possible to my patient." This action aided my efforts to remain mindful of trying to be helpful to my patients.

Realize that you will encounter people who have a wide range of emotions. Mentally prepare yourself to not react negatively to people who are angry or extremely stressed. This is hard to do, at first, but becomes easier with practice.

Try to maintain an attitude of quiet confidence, with some humility. Excessive pride has no good purpose in medicine. Of course, many patients need to be reassured about your capabilities, so it is appropriate to reassure them, as needed. But refrain from arrogance and boasting.

Be completely honest with your patients, or with parents if the patient is a child, or with the parents and child, if the child is old enough to understand his or her situation. If you don't know the answer to their question(s), tell them that you don't know. Let them know whether testing or treatment are needed, or if they can let nature take its course. And if testing or treatment are needed, to what extent are they needed? If two different plans have approximately equal likelihood of being helpful, let the patient and/or parents decide between the two plans. And remember that Jesus taught us not to waste; I think that this can easily apply to not over-utilizing medical resources, both diagnostic and therapeutic.

Be realistic with your patient, or his or her parents, if a good outcome is very unlikely. It is not necessary or even appropriate to be like a cheerleader and advocate doing everything possible to achieve survival when survival is very unlikely or comes with a great decrease in quality of life; doing this can easily be a disservice to your patient and his or her family. Of course, patients and their families are the most important elements when it comes to decision making, but you should provide adequate and honest information and your opinion to help with decision making.

Treat patients with severe neurological and mental impairment, or any other type of disability, with the same respect that you would show to patients without such problems. We don't know how much of what we say and do is perceived and understood by a patient with severe mental impairment. And even if nothing is being sensed by the patient, I think that his or her parent(s) or caregiver appreciate the respect being shown, and I am certain that God appreciates this type of care for His children.

Try to always focus on your patients' needs and not your own needs. Do your best to avoid rushing through visits with patients. Each and every patient is important. Try to remember that meeting the needs of each and every patient is why you practice medicine. If you have to rush through visits with patients, then you need more help. If you have the ability to control your patient load, you should schedule fewer patient visits. Of course, all of this is easier said than done, but please try to do your best to avoid making your patients feel that you don't have adequate time for them or interest in them.

Don't hesitate to pray again, repeatedly, if necessary, for and about your patient, especially if your patient isn't doing well, or you are stumped by his or her problem. Foremost, pray for your patient's health. And pray for the patient and family to have strength and a measure of peace in facing adversity. And please remember that miracles are possible!! And don't hesitate to thank God for good outcomes!

Try to embrace diversity in your patient population. Diversity includes socioeconomic, ethnic, gender identity, racial and religious differences. Remind yourself frequently that every patient that you see was created by God and is important to God! And remember that if the patient is important to God, he or she is important to you! (This might be the most important part of living your faith.)....I think that the greatest experiences and lessons that I had during my more than twenty-six years in pediatric emergency medicine, preceded by over six years in general pediatrics, involved meeting people, learning about people, and learning to try to greatly value each and every patient and my encounters with them.

Anymore I try not to categorize people, but for the sake of making a couple of points, I will, in the following examples.

People on Medicaid. Starting in my medical school days, I noticed that a fair number of health professionals tended to look down on people on Medicaid. I admit that for a number of years, I occasionally shared in having this attitude. Gradually, though, during my pediatric emergency medicine career, I found myself rethinking this attitude more and more. Especially when I started making more of an effort to live my faith at work, I noticed that most of the Medicaid recipients who initially seemed unfriendly would soon lose this attitude and start interacting more warmly with me. I now think that most of them who initially have an unfriendly attitude when in a healthcare setting have that attitude as a result of having had to endure negative attitudes directed at them from healthcare professionals and others. They likely have been repeatedly treated in condescending manners. Wouldn't most or all of us put on hardened attitudes if we were repeatedly treated in this manner?

Sometimes the term "freeloader", or something equivalent, is applied to Medicaid recipients by some healthcare professionals. I think that it is best for everyone, ourselves included, if we get rid of this attitude. We have no way of knowing if someone is a "freeloader." We do not know their life circumstances. We haven't walked in their shoes. Our role as healthcare professionals is not to be judgmental and condescending. Our role is to be as helpful as possible for all of our patients, regardless of their insurance status or lack of insurance. And I'm pretty sure that most presumed "freeloaders" aren't "freeloaders." And, if a few are, so what? We have to remember that we are all "freeloaders", in a sense. God has given all of us more than we will ever give Him!!!

Especially for those of us who call ourselves Christians, I again highly recommend adopting the "what would Jesus do?" approach to interacting with patients and their families, if you haven't already. And, again, even non-Christian healthcare professionals can try this, or they can try practicing according to the most noble aims of their respective faiths. It is heartwarming to see the look of appreciation on peoples' faces when you treat them with kindness and respect, especially when they were initially understandably inclined to be unfriendly.

One more thing on Medicaid. I'm very disappointed in all of the states in which I have ever lived for not expanding Medicaid coverage! Shame on us!

Ethnic, racial and religious diversity. My pediatric emergency medicine career seemed to be one long lesson in racial, ethnic, and religious diversity. I admit that initially I preferred to see people who seemed more like me. As time went on, I realized that it was very enriching (and I don't mean in the monetary sense) for me to meet and interact with people of all racial and ethnic groups and of all faiths. I eventually came to the realization that a high percentage of people belonging to racial, ethnic, and religious minorities that I had the privilege of meeting had endured far worse life circumstances than I ever would. And almost all were extremely respectful, as well as thankful, for the care that my colleagues and I provided them. By the end of my career, I think that I actually preferred meeting people who weren't like me.

My final comments apply to all of us, not just healthcare professionals. We hear or see lots of stories in the news these days about ethnic diversity, immigrants, and related issues. Many of the stories concern the fears that a number of our citizens have regarding immigrants, ethnic diversity, and religious diversity. From my experience, we shouldn't be fearful! Please remember that almost all of us are descendants of immigrants. And also please realize this: if we treat those who are different from us poorly, there almost certainly will be far more problems than if we treat them well. Would our immigrant ancestors be proud of us for our negative attitudes and fears? And more importantly yet, does God look favorably upon us when we have these negative attitudes and fears and don't do our absolute best to overcome them?

Afterthoughts

There is one more item regarding thoughts of some people of one race about the people of another that I feel should be addressed. And this bias isn't necessarily connected to medical professionals, although undoubtedly it plagues some of us. These thoughts concern laziness. I have on rare occasion read that this or that person thinks that people of another race are lazy. These thoughts have troubled me for a long time. I wondered why anyone would think that or say that. Is there any basis for it?

As I thought more of my own situation, depression, it made me wonder if many of those who are perceived as being "lazy" are depressed (I am not qualified to say this definitively; this is speculation only). Many times, I didn't want to go to work. At these times, I simply thought that I was lazy, and I wasn't sure why. Sometimes when my inspiration to go to work was especially low, I would think that I had chosen the wrong profession, but then I couldn't think of anything else that I wanted to do, either. And I enjoyed my work when the demands weren't too great, but very often the demands exceeded my comfort level. What kept me going was inspiration from my wife and family, and the needs of my patients and their families. Income helped also, but after a while it wasn't enough of a motivator. And, for the last half of my career, prayer played an ever-increasing role.

Extrapolating from my own experience made me speculate that perhaps a lot of people who appear to be lazy are actually depressed. And now please consider this question: Don't you think that a person might have a greater likelihood of depression if he or she were part of a group of people who had endured discrimination and hatred on the basis of skin color for hundreds of years?

How to live

Who wants to be told how to live? At first, I thought, almost no one. Isn't it in our nature to want to be in charge of our lives? But then I thought, what about all of the guide books that you can find in bookstores? There is a plethora of books filled with advice and plans for achieving happiness or almost any other desired state. This means that at least some of us want advice on how to live. Perhaps if we are unhappy or feeling unfulfilled, we are more likely to seek this kind of advice. But I think that these are also appropriate considerations for those who feel happy and fulfilled, or at least, think they do. In this chapter, I will briefly cover some of the lifestyle choices that I find helpful.

Take care of your body!

Undoubtedly, you have heard countless times the various ways to do this, so I won't bore you with too much information on that. Just giving you this information again probably wouldn't help much. But maybe providing another way of looking at this issue will be helpful to some who need help. Motivation for some might come from this thought: God wants us to take care of our bodies. He does not want us to abuse our bodies by doing any number of things that we know are unhealthy or unsafe. How do I know this? The Bible gives us information on this. 1 Corinthians 6:19 and 20 say, "What? know ye not that your body is the temple of the Holy Ghost which is in you, which ye have of God, and ye are not your own? For ye are bought with a price: therefore glorify God in your body, and in your spirit, which are God's." To me this means that we should do our very best to stay healthy and avoid harmful behaviors so that we are better able to serve and glorify God, which, incidentally, is also the best way to serve ourselves, in case we are feeling left out of the equation! We stay healthy by adopting lifestyle habits that are healthy. These include the following: avoid overeating and eat a healthy diet, avoid smoking, avoid drug abuse and overconsumption of alcohol, exercise sufficiently and safely on a regular basis, get at least seven to eight hours of sleep nightly, live safely, and keep stress at tolerable levels (Excessive stress in our lives is very unhealthy for our bodies; tending to the items listed above helps reduce stress, and tending to our mental and spiritual health needs also helps with our stress levels. And strongly consider prayer. As I'm fond of saying, it won't hurt and it might help. Actually, I feel more strongly about it than that!)

Live simply!

This not only reduces stress, but it also helps reduce expenses. Try to find pleasure in simple things, like walks in the neighborhood, or conversations with your friends (and those who may become your friends) that you meet while walking. There are many more possibilities. And ignore your "modern devices" while walking. Stress relief from walking is much greater when one "unplugs" from the manmade "things of this world" and tunes in to God's creation.

Live happily!

Try to laugh frequently! This is very helpful for your health (physical, mental, and spiritual).

Allow yourself to cry when needed

God created our ability to cry for a reason. I think that it is a stress reliever for us, and, by relieving stress, it probably actually helps us to live more happily.

Try to find truly meaningful ways to feel positive about yourself.

Do not try to use wealth or the objects it can buy for this purpose! If you are blessed with wealth you should enjoy it, but you should also keep it in proper perspective. Be thankful for it, but do not flaunt it. And please share some of your good fortune with the less fortunate. Finding ways of helping others is probably the best way to achieve this goal. And be careful to not be too proud of your efforts; simply let the joy of interacting with others and helping them be your reward.

Allow yourself to be more impressed by God's creations than man's creations

Keep track of the changes in the flora and fauna, as well as overall scenery, on your walks or bike rides. Pay attention to the sounds of nature. Appreciate the wonderful feel of a gentle breeze. And so on. And so on. (A pair of Bible verses that I like come to mind. They are Matthew 6:28 and 29. In them, Jesus is making a different point than I am attempting to make, but you can probably see why I include them. They say, ".......Consider the lilies of the field, how they grow; they toil not, neither do they spin: And yet I say unto you, That even Solomon in all his glory was not arrayed like one of these.")

Take advantage of opportunities to socialize with family and friends, as well as with others who might become friends

And do this in a safe manner, of course. Like laughter, this is beneficial for your health (obviously, these areas overlap).

Share meals with your family as often as possible, and with as few distractions as possible

This should be a time for civilized conversation, laughter, appreciating God's gifts to us, etc., so avoid things like books and electronic devices at the table. Good eye contact is essential. A good example of this activity can regularly be found on the CBS series Blue Bloods.

Address any mental health needs

Often, just doing the things that I address here is all the help needed for feeling stressed or slightly depressed. If you need more help, consult your doctor, or someone else who is qualified to help you. No one needs to be missing out on the joys of life!

Try to help the less fortunate!

You know as well as I do that there are lots of ways to do this. And there is probably more need for this now than ever before.

Waste not!

This is common sense, but now I have a much greater appreciation for this after recently reading of a request that Jesus made, which can be found in the book of John, after the story of one of His miracles, the feeding of the five thousand. John 6:12 says, "when they were filled, He said unto His disciples, 'Gather up the fragments that remain, that nothing be lost.'" To me, this is a powerful message to us that we shouldn't waste! That this message came from Jesus, who could have created any amount of food that He wanted, makes it all the more powerful!!

Live in a manner that benefits your descendants and others in their generation(s).

Set good examples for them. Try to save some of your money so that they have an inheritance, in case times will become more difficult. This will help them to be able to meet their needs, and it will also help them to be able to help others who are less fortunate. And live in a manner that is beneficial to the environment, especially in regard to global warming; this is also an excellent way to help countless other people!! The Union of Concerned Scientists (UCS) has great advice in this area. Consider becoming a financial supporter of UCS. If you are skeptical about, or flat-out disagree with, this part of my advice, I ask (as humbly as possible) that you start reading science information that has not been filtered by a political party or by the executives of carbon-based energy companies. For those of us who are concerned about adverse climate change from global warming, we should act like we are concerned! We should quit buying gas-guzzling cars and trucks, we should live closer to our work, if possible, and we should look for other ways to reduce our carbon footprint. For those of us who don't feel this is important, I ask that we periodically detach ourselves from our disregard of science and ask ourselves, "What if there really is something to the concerns of climate scientists? Do I really want my descendants to think very poorly of me for not doing my part?" (If we knew that the Second Appearance of Jesus on earth will be in the next few years, then this issue probably isn't as important. But we don't know that! For the sake of the health of the earth, we should live as if our climate-friendly efforts will truly matter!)

Beware of financial pressure!

My initial thought on this, years ago, when I started using this expression, was that financial pressure was a situation in which one had lots of money, maybe too much. Now I think that financial pressure can be either positive financial pressure or negative financial pressure. I will define each so that you know what I mean by financial pressure. Positive financial pressure is the situation in which having lots of money, or possibly too much money, makes one want to do something that someone in his or her right mind wouldn't consider doing (such as, buying a two-million-dollar toy). Negative financial pressure is the situation in which having too little money makes one want to do something that someone in his or her right mind wouldn't consider doing (such as, robbing a bank). Of course, lots of us (me included) aspire to have positive financial pressure, but we must be well prepared for this when and if it appears in our lives so that this situation doesn't ruin us (damage our faith or interpersonal relationships, for example).

Try to live within your means!

Obviously, this is related to financial pressure. This can be difficult if one has a low paying job. But I think that it is a worthy goal, and it helps one avoid excessive stress. If one can't or won't live within one's means, one has the tendency to get a second, or third, job. The resulting lack of time off and lack of adequate rest is highly stressful, and is detrimental to a person's physical, mental, and spiritual health. That is why I am in favor of minimum wage increases for all the people who have to rely on minimum wage jobs to meet their families' needs. Incidentally, their work is just as honorable as the work of someone who makes any amount more than what they do, and often it is more honorable!

Live as if you are at the end of your life, and also live as if you have many years remaining!

The first part refers to the need to have your faith in order, since, as my mother was fond of saying, "you never know what's in a day!" And the second part helps us to feel like fully embracing life, having goals, and being productive in many ways, including spiritually. And together they also help us to avoid delay in doing these things. This helps us to feel vital and also helps us to avoid depression.

Keep the faith!

My recommendation, of course, is that you keep the same faith that I do. But if you are not inspired to do so, keep the faith that you have, but test it periodically, being open to finding out more about my faith if you lack abundant inspiration, love, hope, and joy in your own faith.

Live according to this question, "What would Jesus do?"

(And don't approach this with the idea of finding out what Jesus would do just so you can do the opposite of what He would do!) How do we know what Jesus would do? Read the Gospels, especially the part called the Beatitudes. Then, start "living your faith" based on His examples and teachings. Of course, we are humans, and this is hard for us. We will never be as good at this as Jesus was, but we don't have the advantages that He did (He had a couple of distinct advantages over us when it came to the ability to "live as Jesus would". One, He Was Jesus; that helped a lot. Second, He was the Son of God the Father; that helped even more!). But one of His purposes in joining humanity was to teach us how to live by His examples and His words, and we should strive to follow His examples and His words. Again, it won't hurt, and there is a high likelihood that it will help!

Incidentally, until recently, I didn't have the courage to fully embrace the idea of promoting living according to the question "what would Jesus do?" Ever since I first heard of it many years ago, I thought that it was a great idea, but promoting it was an entirely different matter. It certainly wasn't convenient, and it seemed as if would be an embarrassing thing for me to do. Now, after more fully embracing my faith, I am comfortable with writing about it. And I'm pretty sure that I am now comfortable talking about it, too.

The Prescription

In the medical field, prescriptions concisely apply to what a patient needs for his or her health to be restored or preserved. In this part, I list the things that I believe are needed for the restoration and preservation of our eternal spiritual health. These things include a few actions for us to take, as well as the basic, core beliefs that we should hold.

What follows is my Faith Prescription.

The important actions for us to take are to love God; to know that God loves you; to make God number one in your life; to live your faith according to the examples of Jesus, keeping in mind the question, "What would Jesus do? (especially His command to love your neighbor as yourself)"; and to try to transform your faith into the "faith of a child".

The core beliefs that we should have are that God is Triune (God the Father, God the Son [Jesus], and God the Holy Spirit). While He was on earth, Jesus was both God and man. Our goal is to be with God in eternity. To be with God in eternity we must have salvation from the wages of our sins. Eternal damnation is what we, by ourselves, earn from living our sinful lives. We are all sinful and have fallen short of the glory of God. The price of our salvation has already been paid by Jesus' suffering and death on the cross, the completion of His suffering in hell[6], and His resurrection

---

[6] Not all theologians agree with this. This is what I learned during catechism studies, and there is a Bible verse that refers to Jesus being in hell. The verse is Acts 2:31. In this verse, Peter is speaking of David in his role as a prophet. The words of this verse are, "He seeing this before spake of the resurrection of Christ, that his soul was not left in hell, neither did his flesh see corruption." Furthermore, even though it is all speculation, my idea in Physics of Faith is that it makes more sense that Jesus would have to suffer in hell, as a deity, to be able to suffer enough for the salvation of all who will be saved, than it does for His only suffering to have been on the cross. But, I suppose, it is adequate for us to know that whatever suffering He did was sufficient, according to the plan of God the Father, for our salvation.

from the dead. We receive salvation from the wages of our sin when we believe in God (God the Father, God the Son, and God the Holy Spirit), know that God the Son (Jesus) has already paid the price for our salvation, know that we have no means of salvation other than through our faith in Jesus (salvation isn't attained by doing good works), confess our sins, and be penitent for our sins (Please remember the line from the movie Indiana Jones and the Last Crusade, "Only the penitent man will pass.").

If you read this and don't agree with what I have written, please strongly consider doing the following: periodically read, with an open mind, the words of Jesus in the New Testament, and pray earnestly and honestly to God for inspiration and enlightenment about the faith that He wants you to have, and see where He leads you. And if you read this and do agree with what I have written, please pray earnestly and often for the preservation and strengthening of your faith. Amen!

Afterwords

Toward a full disclosure

The title was chosen because I will never get to a full disclosure. There will likely always be something to add to the list of disclosures. I like to think of this disclosure section as an invitation to you, the reader, to think about influences in your own life. As part of this introspection it is absolutely appropriate and beneficial to look for the influence(s) of God in your own life, either directly or through other people who interact with you.

For my readers who happen to be politicians, I like to think that this section is an invitation for you to be open to changing your mind about issues. Please do this as necessary to work for the greatest possible benefit for people. Please remember that you represent all of your constituents, not just the people who voted for you!

Disclosure 1

In the story, Safe Arrival at Church, in the part entitled Near Misses, I told you that one of the hymns that I played at church was Crown Him with Many Crowns. I was certain of this until a few months ago, when our church's bells concert included the hymn All Hail the Power of Jesus' Name. All of the verses of this hymn, apart from one alternate verse, end with the line "and crown Him lord of all." I still think that my story includes the correct hymn. However, now I sometimes wonder, "Did I play both hymns in that service?"

And ever since the time that I first heard All Hail the Power of Jesus' Name in the bells concert, I have occasionally wondered whether a bells concert would ever include both hymns. Well, it finally happened during the summer of 2016. When I heard the beginning of the second of the two hymns, I felt the hairs on my arms raise. I wasn't sure if it (both hymns being played in the same concert) meant anything, and I'm still not sure, but two days later I decided that it might mean something, which I will now reveal in Disclosure 2.

Disclosure 2

I took the awaited pairing of hymns as a sign that I was nearly finished with my writing for this project. How did I arrive at this thought? Just before the bells concert I had begun thinking about writing some disclosures to include in this book. At that point, I had been thinking of A Full Disclosure for the title. Two days later, with effortless thought, I reversed the word order of the two key words and changed one of them to arrive at this phrase: the disclosure of fullness. I then thought, "That's it! My book is full! (I know some of you are thinking, "It's full of it, alright!"). I'm nearly done! Oh, Yahoo!" (Actually, I had known that I was close to being finished, but I was contemplating writing about one additional topic. But I was having a hard time getting adequate inspiration for that topic, so I was indeed very happy with my disclosure of fullness!)

Disclosure 3

I wrote most of this book while under the influence of music. I listened to lots of classical and baroque music, guitar music, and Mannheim Steamroller's Fresh Aire series. I don't listen to a lot of vocal music because of my hearing impairment, but I found that listening to Sarah Brightman's Classics was especially inspirational. I greatly enjoy all of the Fresh Aire CDs, but I found the most helpful one for my writing was Fresh Aire V, especially the part entitled Dancin' In The Stars. The guitar CDs that I found most helpful were Bella Luna and the Train to San Lorenzo by Michael Petrovich and Archguitar Renaissance by Peter Blanchette......It seems that music greases the path for words to get from my brain to the computer screen, somewhat like the effect that wax had on Clark Griswold's sled in the classic comedy National Lampoon's Christmas Vacation.

Disclosure 4

I didn't get as much reading done as I wanted to during the months that I worked on this project, but I did manage to get two books read. They were The Vicar of Christ, by Walter F. Murphy, and The Watchmaker of Filigree Street, by Natasha Pulley. I selected these books simply because they looked interesting to me, but many times, as I was reading them, I thought, "Was I inspired to choose these books to help with my project?"

Disclosure 5

Earlier I told you about my favorite dream, which I call my "flying dream." I complained that I hadn't had the dream for a long time. I'm happy to say that this dream made a reappearance on August 16, 2016, just before midnight (I woke briefly, right after my dream, and noted that the time was 11:55 PM). My wife and I were traveling, and this was our first night on the road. I remember that before falling asleep I had prayed for a good night of sleep, since I do the driving.

To my knowledge, this was the first time that I had my favorite dream in 2016. It differed from the usual version, however. In this most recent version, part of the time I felt like I was flying and part of the time I felt as though I was cheering for someone else who was flying. The action seemed to go back and forth between me being the flyer and me being the cheerer. On the ground were many people who were trying to reach up and grab the flyer, whether it was me or the person for whom I was cheering. The people seemed intent on hindering our efforts, or possibly they wanted to discover how we were able to fly. Or both. Regardless of who was flying, the flyer was always just out of reach of the people on the ground.

I now like to think that the flyer for whom I was cheering was you, the reader!

Disclosure 6

Regarding depression, I still feel "it" at times, but it is minor and very manageable. The feeling goes away if I simply get busy with something. Prayer and contemplation of the goodness of God are also very helpful. It is minor enough now that it is more of a gift than a problem. I sometimes think of it as God's way of telling me to get busy, since there is much to be done in our world.

And concerning the severity of depression, probably a person who didn't know he was depressed is a poor judge of its severity.

Disclosure 7

I have no regrets about using my personal memories of my parents' relationship and my brother's depression. I think that the memories of the deceased are most useful if they can be a force for good, and I think that some good can be derived from sharing my family memories. Writing about these memories made me feel even more strongly that

I wouldn't trade my family, or my "growing up" years, for anyone else's, even if I could do so! I am very comfortable that my parents and brother welcome my use of their memories for the purposes of this book.

Disclosure 8

From my current perspective (very shortly before publication), I now feel that my career was absolutely the right one for me. I do think that I had a true passion for my work, but that passion was opposed by the effects of depression. And I now think that if I had it all to do over again, I would end up in the same role, a pediatric emergency physician. And if God for some reason inspired me (and made it possible for me) to do it over again, I would have two requests of Him: 1) that I would be blessed with my current insights going forward, and 2) that I would be empowered by an even stronger faith, always keeping in mind God's words of empowerment from Philippians 4:13, "I can do all things through Christ who strengthens me." (NKJV).

Whom would I like to meet?

President Obama and his entire family

During President Obama's terms in office I would often hear negative comments about him from some of my friends. I haven't seen what they see. To me, our former president, Barack Obama, his wife, Michelle, and their daughters, Malia and Sasha, are one of the classiest families in America! President Obama was, and still is, a pillar of dignity and grace despite having had to endure, for most of his presidency, uncooperative congressional leadership (to put it mildly!). And I think that all of the members of our former First Family are wonderful role models for the people of our nation.

If I ever had the opportunity to meet the Obama family, I would have some objectives for the meeting, apart from simply the great pleasure of meeting them. My challenge to our former president might be one of his greatest challenges ever. It would be to teach a shy, hearing impaired, mediocre singer how to sing the first verse of Amazing Grace like he does! And I would like to hear the future plans of each of them, including those of Sasha and Malia.

(Actually, I would also like to meet all of our former presidents and their wives).

Former Speaker of the House John Boehner

Despite rarely agreeing with him politically, I kind of admire him. He is eloquent, and he is better behaved than a lot of the newer faces in his party. Incidentally, his party was my party until last year (although I was a RINO); now I'm registered as an Independent. But the main reason that

I would like to meet him is that he is the "poster child" for men with our mutual "gift." In case you are still wondering what our mutual "gift" is, go back to Reflections on spigotology.

If we ever had the opportunity to meet, I imagine that we would do a series of manly things, such as shaking hands, hugging, talking about our "gifts", especially about what sets them off, demonstrating our "gifts", and then shaking hands again, followed by hugging again, before going our separate ways.

Chancellor Angela Merkel

For years, I have admired her for her thoughtful and effective leadership in Germany. And her influence in helping to stabilize the European Union economically is worthy of respect. Even more recently, my level of admiration for her has further increased with her compassionate and courageous response to the plight of vast numbers of refugees.

The world would greatly benefit from more leaders like her. She probably would have been a good or even a great leader as a man, but I think that as a woman she has a leadership advantage because she doesn't suffer from the affliction of "testosterone poisoning." Women generally cooperate better than men to get needed things accomplished. This ability is very helpful in government, in my opinion.

And on a more personal level, she is now a role model for me. She has successfully transitioned from a career as a scientist to a career as a government leader. Her example gives me inspiration for my own transition from a career in a science-related profession to my current role, however long or short, as a Judeo-Christian writer.

Prime Minister Justin Trudeau

As with Angela Merkel, I greatly admire and respect his welcoming attitude toward refugees.

There are undoubtedly other leaders whom I have failed to mention but who respond with compassion to refugees. But there are far too many who respond in an unwelcoming manner. In the U.S., we are divided on this issue, and as a result, we aren't as helpful to refugees as we could be, and we aren't fully living up to the symbolism of the Statue of Liberty. If this continues, the Statue of Liberty might be more appropriately located in another harbor, such as that of Hamburg, Vancouver, Toronto, Montreal, or any of several other great cities. I prefer that it remain where it is, but I also would like us to live up to the words of Emma Lazarus' poem, The New Colossus, that is found on a plaque inside of the pedestal of the statue:

Not like the brazen giant of Greek fame,
With conquering limbs astride from land to land;
Here at our sea-washed, sunset gates shall stand
A mighty woman with a torch, whose flame
Is the imprisoned lightning, and her name
Mother of Exiles. From her beacon-hand
Glows world-wide welcome; her mild eyes command
The air-bridged harbor that twin cities frame.
"Keep ancient lands, your storied pomp!" cries she
With silent lips. "Give me your tired, your poor,
Your huddled masses yearning to breathe free,
The wretched refuse of your teeming shore.
Send these, the homeless, tempest-tost to me,
I lift my lamp beside the golden door!"

I recommend that all of us read more about refugees, especially those of us who have fears about them. The website for We Welcome Refugees (especially the FAQs) is an excellent resource.

The Child and Her Mom, plus RN, from the Miracle? Story

Now that I am taking this story more seriously, I would like to go through the story again from the mom's perspective and from RN's perspective. And, of course, I would like to meet the grown-up version of the patient in the story.

The University of Nebraska Men's and Women's Basketball Teams

I would like to meet each of these teams just after each has won a semifinal game in their respective NCAA Tournaments. Do you think I am dreaming? Remember, I have faith!!

What's next?

Until early Fall of 2016, I didn't know if I would do any more writing, but I did realize that I was open to inspiration. But now, God willing, it appears that there will be a second book.

Some good words

Here are some good farewell words to keep in mind until we meet again, whether in person or in print, no matter when and where our next meeting will be, in this world, or in the realm of eternity. They are from Numbers 6:24–26.

The Lord bless thee and keep thee:
The Lord make His face shine upon thee and be gracious unto thee:
The Lord lift up His countenance upon thee and give thee peace.

www.ingramcontent.com/pod-product-compliance
Lightning Source LLC
Chambersburg PA
CBHW071314060426
42444CB00036B/2714